RESTORING
LEBANON

Also by Nizar Y. Younes

Resala Ela Alma (Letter to Alma) Beirut, 2007, Dar An-Nahar for Publishing and Distribution

Barlaman al-Ghad (The Parliament of Tomorrow) Beirut, 2006, Dar al-Masar Publishing House

Attariq Ela Addawala (The Road to the State) Beirut, 2004, Dar al-Masar Publishing House

Lubnan al-Akhar (The Other Lebanon) Beirut, 2000, Dar al-Masar Publishing House

RESTORING LEBANON

Nizar Y. Younes

RESTORING LEBANON

iUniverse books may be ordered through booksellers or by contacting:

iUniverse
1663 Liberty Drive
Bloomington, IN 47403
www.iuniverse.com
1-800-Authors (1-800-288-4677)

Because of the dynamic nature of the Internet, any web addresses or
links contained in this book may have changed since publication and
may no longer be valid. The views expressed in this work are solely those
of the author and do not necessarily reflect the views of the publisher,
and the publisher hereby disclaims any responsibility for them.

Any people depicted in stock imagery provided by Thinkstock are models,
and such images are being used for illustrative purposes only.
Certain stock imagery © Thinkstock.

ISBN: 978-1-5320-2366-8 (sc)
ISBN: 978-1-5320-2367-5 (hc)
ISBN: 978-1-5320-2365-1 (e)

Library of Congress Control Number: 2017911699

Print information available on the last page.

iUniverse rev. date: 03/14/2018

Contents

Preface

For the past fifty years I have been traipsing across cities, countries, and deserts, toting my carryall, my files, and various project schemes. I've been teaching, learning, and visiting my colleagues in branch offices and on project sites, seeking to build a better world for the sake of humankind—a world of peace, beauty, and goodness.

During my life I have known neither boredom nor monotony. I have loved my profession as well as mathematics. I have cherished my colleagues—as well as companions and even their children—who toil in foreign cities and remote deserts. I hold dear my ancestral tales, my village, and my family's land, "Ayn el-Haffe," which I have landscaped with lakelets, trees, and flowers. I have been elated by the poetry of Said Akl, Badr Shakir al-Sayyab, and Mahmoud Darwish and by Fairuz's heavenly singing.

I love Lebanon, the country to which we lay claim, the country whose role we have yet to understand, the country where our responsibilities are yet to be reset.

I like to dream of a republic that measures up to the love I have for this country, a love to which I dedicate the remainder of my days.

My neighbor Tanios in Ayn el-Haffe was a simple, witty farmer. I never met him without him whispering in my ear, "So when will Lebanon be back? I shall not marry and have a family until it returns."

My friend Khalid from the Gulf also loves Lebanon and reproaches all Lebanese for denying him "heaven on earth." Like Tanios, Khalid is still waiting, shaking his head, ruefully saying, "The more time goes by, the more we feel how badly we need Lebanon. Whoever doesn't miss Lebanon is not an Arab at heart."

Before the tragic events of the Arab Spring, the Syrian and Arab cultural elites were waiting for a Lebanese Spring. They reflected a commonly held view that the declining Arab societies had no real chance of a new renaissance or liberation from backwardness and autocracy unless Lebanon were to regain the traditional role it played in the renaissance of the Arab Mashreq (the region of the Arab world to the east of Egypt, which comprises Lebanon, Palestine, Jordan, Syria, and Iraq). They waited for a Lebanese Spring to provide the Arab world with a model of a democratic, secular republic that fosters freedom and culture, embraces diversity, and is committed to modernity.

Before being rudely awakened, most Western intellectuals and politicians were confident of their dogmatic assumption that a clash of civilizations would inevitably occur, resulting in the triumph of the superior Western civilization. They believed Western civilization would be sufficiently hearty to absorb and assimilate the identities of immigrants, instead of ignoring or excluding their particularities.

European countries have now woken to a transformation that has overtaken the demography of their cities. Since the mid-twentieth century, immigrants, refugees, and other foreigners have moved into European countries. Western thinkers have been forced to review their assumptions and critically examine the grave problematics stemming from their disregard for the religious and cultural diversity that has taken hold within their quarters.

Interestingly, the Lebanese laboratory of living together,[1] which had long ago fallen out of respect and been forgotten, has diffidently returned to the attention of Western intellectuals searching for the roots of civilization's backwardness and inability to deal with unfettered, impulsive violence and the lust to negate others. Western intellectuals have discovered that our country, despite having had its role crippled amid attempts to destabilize and plunder it, remains the most suitable testing ground for an embrace of diversity toward the realization of a culture of living together, not only for the countries of the Arab Mashreq but for the entire world.

Despite the dangers surrounding Lebanon, Lebanese elites have begun to assume responsibility for the consequences of their failure to fulfill the role they have chosen for their country. They are increasingly convinced that Lebanon's return to its former values and role is a critical need for all of human civilization, especially Western countries that have snubbed small Lebanon and left it to its own devices to contend with the fate that has been imposed on it.

This belief that Lebanon's uniqueness and distinctive features qualify its people to play an effective role in bridging, cross-pollinating, and harmonizing civilizations reflects a trend in global public opinion that gained popularity in the second half of the twentieth century in cultural circles and international organizations. It was expressed by René Maheu, a former director general of UNESCO. Writing about the Lebanese tragedy for *Le Monde* (November 20, 1975), he concluded with this splendid insight: "These features embody the essence of civilization itself. They are not so common that we should accept the drying up of

---

[1] The author emphasizes employing the term "living together," not "coexistence." He considers Lebanon as a model for creating an environment where people from different religions can live in harmony.

their wellsprings in the place that can most assuredly provide them in abundance."

The present is no longer an extension of the past. For the first time in the course of Lebanon's civilization, we are seeing a break that has placed us on the threshold of a new age, though an age whose features remain hazy and unclear. The role of a crisis-beset Lebanon, which is likewise unclear and has not yet come into focus, will depend on our awareness of the problem of our booby-trapped, shackled reality. It will depend on whether we have the courage to liberate ourselves from the prison of our religious communities and unavoidable mutual suspicions. We have inadvertently been thrust into this prison.

Lebanon's role in the world has been neutralized. During this critical period in human history, our country has been transformed into a yoke on the world when it could have been a critically essential laboratory of living together, one that might have showcased the capacities of individuals to become free of their primitive instincts and tribalism and instead adhere to the intellectual streams and sublime humanitarian values that unify modern societies.

Lebanese politicians often seem almost schizophrenic. In their rhetoric, they criticize the sectarian political system, all the while entrenching and legitimizing it. There must be a responsible, succinct answer to the question as to whether Lebanese people are able and determined to live together in a secular republic free of sectarian loyalties and affiliations, and whether the Lebanese religious communities wish to reclaim their role as spiritual and cultural entities and stay out of political conflicts. These questions, which have persisted since the sectarian political system first arose, remain unanswered.

States are neither eternal nor abstract realities. Rather, they embody the will of a people at a given time and place to join efforts to achieve prosperity and happiness for all its members. The state's failure to achieve these objectives necessitates looking for the root defect. The defect cannot be in the nation, since everyone is equally attached to it. Nor can we blame Lebanese individuals, who excel in their morals; are strong in their character, backbone, and perseverance; and are open and tolerant. Without these characteristics the state would not have survived. Thus there should be an outright dismissal of the absurd claims casting doubt on the innate nature of the Lebanese and saying it is backward, corrupt, and egotistical; such claims would distract attention from who or what is truly responsible for our decline.

In political science the state has three constituents: the nation, the people, and the political system. If the problem does not lie within our nation or people, it must lie within our universally condemned (at least in public) sectarian political system. It is only natural that the sectarian division of the state would fuel the struggle between the religious communities over their respective shares of power. This struggle leads willy-nilly to a sectarian balance of power that is constantly shifting according to domestic and foreign alliances or changes. The ultimate result is a slide toward tensions, conflicts, and periodic civil wars. If it is not possible or expected to exchange our nation for another nation or our people for another people, our only option is to replace our inherently defective sectarian political system.

The legitimacy of that system was originally derived from an implicit contract inspired by culture, tradition, and ad hoc covenants growing out of the memory of coexistence and the common suffering and struggle for survival, which has implanted values such as freedom, tolerance, solidarity, and openness to dialogue among the Lebanese Unfortunately, the contract regulating the way in which we are to live together remains fuzzy. Its terms are open to contradictory interpretations and are thus unsuited to serving as recognized terms of reference for resolving conflicts that arise among sectarian groups. Therein lies the defect.

Politics, which is derived from the Greek word *politika,* meaning "affairs of the cities," is usually practiced according to a specific system and set of rules, by which a governing authority is formed and discharges its responsibilities in regard to economic growth, security, and cultural advancement. The success or failure of any political system depends on its competence in the management of relations among the different components that govern the frameworks of life. The political system strives to minimize contradictions and provide for the coordination and interaction of the different components in order to survive and thrive, just as any living organism must have all of its body parts functioning in order to stay alive and flourish. The impairment of any component of the political system necessarily imbalances the system and neutralizes its effectiveness. To minimize contradictions or deficiencies, there should exist, as terms of reference, a social contract between the entities comprising the nation or society. Such a contract must set forth fundamental mutual obligations concerning living together among the citizens or groups seeking to coexist in a unified nation.

The social contract provides the contracting parties with imperative rules to resolve claims and conflicting interests, objectives, or viewpoints. It may be possible for a social contract to be implicit in nations whose peoples have a shared culture and shared values. However, a social contract is not an option for a nation that is religiously and culturally diverse; it is a survival imperative whereby a clear, unambiguous charter or covenant is required, which is written, fair, permanent, and recognized.

Confessionalism[2] was born in the mid-nineteenth century, when the country was exposed to incidents reflecting conflicts among foreign powers at the time, as well as to attempts by these powers to exert their influence over the legacy of the Ottoman Empire. This situation continued throughout the French Mandate and after it ended in 1943, as the parties or communities in our pluralistic society evasively neglected to recognize the diversity of Lebanese society, due to their conjectural interests, external alliances, and sectarian schemes. These parties attempted to keep the foundations of the national partnership ambiguous, making do with vague declarations of intentions that have been open to contention, varying interpretations, and deviations.

We claim to live in a democratic republic that is supposed to guarantee its religious communities equal rights, duties, and opportunities as the foundation of its democratic system, yet we avoid asking confusing questions that have no answers in the absence of a reference covenant providing a vital frame as a condition for living together. The willful disregard of, and confusion surrounding, such questions is the origin of the disorder of the communitarian system (a philosophy that emphasizes the connection between the individual and the community) and the direct cause of its failure.

The questions we don't ask include: Who are the contracting parties forming the base of a democracy in the communitarian system? Are they the religious authorities belonging to the eighteen

---

[2]   In Lebanon, confessionalism is a system of government that encourages power sharing among different religious sects through allocating for each a certain proportion within political institutions. In Arabic, confessionalism is known as "*nitham al muhassassat al taifiyyah*"— نظام المحاصصة الطائفية. The proponents of this system see that it secures a peaceful coexistence of the diverse religious communities, whereas critics of confessionalism perceive that it actually deepens conflict among them.

different recognized religious groups[3] in Lebanon? What is the legal definition of a confessional community? What norms has the sectarian system adopted to ensure equality among the sectarian communities? How large is the power share of each community? How can conflicts over power shares be avoided when the size of shares cannot be specified as long as the balances of power are constantly shifting, resulting in inevitable disputes? If the religious community is the basis of the democratic edifice, who will represent it, its spiritual leaders, or its influential politicians? What is the mechanism for choosing the representatives of the community? What is the means of avoiding internal conflict between competing leaders? How is it possible to avoid corrupting the spirituality of the religious community; distorting its cultural spiritual message; and drowning it in egotistic, clientelistic leadership and demagogic conflicts?

None of these questions has an answer, and they lead to other questions. If religious communities are the basis of the democratic edifice, they will represent their members and act on behalf of them in their relations with the authorities. Can we then complain that citizens have a weak sense of citizenship? How does modern political science define citizen? Is someone a citizen of a state or of a religious community? What is the legal definition of a citizen in the political sectarian system?

The confusion between the citizen and his religious community inevitably corrupts democracy. It is obviously impossible to create a democratic political system if citizens are not the foundation of

---

[3]   The present Lebanese Constitution officially acknowledges eighteen religious groups. These have the right to handle family law according to their own courts and traditions, and they are the basic players in Lebanon's complex sectarian politics. They are Alawite, Armenian Catholic, Armenian Orthodox, Assyrian Church of the East, Chaldean Catholic, Copts, Druze, Greek Orthodox, Isma'ili, Jewish, Latin Catholic, Maronite Catholic, Melkite Greek Catholic, Protestant, Sunni, Shia, Syriac Catholic, and Syriac Orthodox.

this democracy. A democracy cannot be created if the concerned state does not have an authoritative covenant that embodies its own values and safeguards the right of citizens to equality and equal opportunity regardless of sectarian identity and affiliation and of the obligation to preserve the natural right for religious groups to difference and protection and liberty. The right of all individuals to equality and equal opportunity is considered a cornerstone of public order, which takes precedence over the principle of sovereignty of the people and the opinion of the majority or the minority in the hierarchy of legal norms.

The Lebanese political establishment has no answer to these questions—not because it is ignorant or lacks insight but because it is corrupt and has clung selfishly to the sectarian quota system under which the country is divided among religious communities' prominent leaderships. Sectarianism became more fiercely entrenched during the period between the establishment of the State of Greater Lebanon in 1920 and the 1989 Taif Agreement. Moreover, its devastating effect has only increased since the conclusion of the Taif Agreement, which has largely remained ink on paper. Where is the answer?

The Lebanese believed that the state selected to exercise the mandate on their devastated and starved country following the end of World War I embodied the values of modernity. They expected that these values would be incorporated in the constitution of the emerging Lebanese state. They believed the mandate authority was keen on harmonizing the new state with the spiritual and moral values of the Lebanese people, and with Lebanon's cultural heritage, as the country sought modernity a humanitarian identity to liberate it from its obscurant Ottoman legacy.

With the declaration of the constitution in 1926, the republic moved away from modernity. The secular republic that embraced the intellectual renaissance launched by the Lebanese in the Middle East was replaced by a republic dedicated to dividing up the country among religious communities (in a throwback to before the French Revolution, and before there were nations or citizenship). True, the Constitution recognized the temporary nature of the confessional political system.

Moreover, it is unlikely that Michel Chiha, the chairman of the committee that drafted the Constitution, was aware that this system would become a destructive, cardinal sin that would stay with us as long as we were unable to free ourselves from sectarian illusions and impulses, and to liberate our decision making from the hegemony of sectarian leaders desperate to defend the spoils provided by the confessional apportionment system (a system of government that refers to de jure mix of religion and politics that typically entails distributing political and institutional power proportionally among confessional communities), which continues to happily reign.

The declaration of the clinical death of the confessional apportionment system at the Taif conference was an illusion. This confessional system reemerged in the garb of the so-called "consensus democracy" (the application of consensus decision making to the process of legislation in a democracy). It continues to seek legitimacy in order to justify its complete disregard of the Taif Agreement (see chapter 1). It has used the current growth of Jihadist extremism to arouse fear and apprehension and to rehabilitate the sectarian ideology and illusory claims that confessionalism—a failed, corrupt system—best protects the religious communities' rights, which are vulnerable to diminishment or encroachment. The very political establishment that had inflamed discord and had repeatedly changed hands as the various parties sought to eliminate each other had the gall to claim that it could remake itself and reclaim legitimacy as the protector of sectarian minorities.

The mass madness that swept through Lebanese society during the 1975–90 civil war was less an expression of latent sectarian hatred than of the suppressed existential anxiety of individuals in dealing with their unfair marginalization and feelings of exclusion under an impotent professional political establishment. In order to purify our memory, lest we use it to rekindle fears, we must first recognize that the impulsive violence of the Civil War was largely directed at others, not at members of another religious community. Likewise, the barbaric violence perpetrated within religious communities actually exceeded the violence that they perpetrated against each other. No religious community was spared fierce infighting.

Despite the terrifying resurgence of violence in the Arab world, which has spread to some parts of Lebanon, I continue to believe that confessionalism is not a dominant or fixed sociological trait of the Lebanese. It is an exterior shell of fear and mistrust of the other. It will dissolve when individuals are able to think clearly and once society has been freed from the toxicity generated by the backward sectarian system. This belief, which contradicts the assumptions generated by prevalent misgivings about the intentions of other religious communities, did not arise in a vacuum. Nor does it reflect utopian desires. Rather, it is the outcome of my personal experience in a life that has been filled with events and enriched by firsthand experiences.

In the introduction to my book, *Barlaman al-Ghad (The Parliament of Tomorrow)*, published in Arabic in 2004 by Dar al-Massar, I relate my first encounter with the other. I was a boarding school student in ninth grade at the Aintoura School. We were assigned to write an essay. I was taken aback by the lack of enthusiasm by my best friend, Nazir Houssami, when I read aloud the essay at the request of the teacher, Milad Salamah, on Independence Day:

> In the essay that I wrote for Independence Day, I expressed the sentiments I perceived in my environment at the time. My friend Nazir Houssami was notably silent. He later told me about the sentiments in his environment. He said

there was a feeling that the Christians, especially the Maronites, were monopolizing political power.

There are many important events that I have experienced in my fast-paced life that I may no longer remember. But nothing had a greater influence on the evolution of my convictions and the orientations of my thinking than those sincere, innocent words said by my schoolmate Nazir when we were not yet fifteen years old.

My friend's words did not erupt like a volcano or set off a storm. Rather, they filtrated quietly, flowing like rivulets that eventually formed a river. I plunged into this river, seeking lost cardinal values and the real meaning of such principles as truth, justice, and equality, which we all claimed but did not fully understand. I bathed in the waters of this river to become purged of the filth of what we imagined to be a social consciousness, which was but a consciousness seeking our own sectarian self.

This incident made me realize early on that the sectarian confessional system was responsible for the feeling that must assail groups that experience inequality and affront to their dignity. It prompted me to rethink the ideas, fears, and myths that were prevalent in my own social environment. It pushed me to listen to others in order to understand their ideas and acknowledge their rights to equality, justice, and human dignity. It allowed me to more precisely appraise the reasons that undermined the enterprise of the Lebanese nation, prompted the emigration of its vital forces, and poisoned national life after the train of the republic forged ahead in the wrong direction, away from the enterprise (or undertaking) that would have granted the Lebanese nation its legitimacy and raison d'etre.

My early liberation from the sectarian ideology led me to abandon the illusion prevailing within each religious community, namely that the sectarian ideology had taken control of the minds of the other religious communities, and to embark on an attempt with a number of my university classmates to unify students from different universities in a single student union notwithstanding the differences in their religious affiliation.

I was fated to have my first participation in national activism on the eve of the bloody 1958 revolution, which ended when the sectarian parties reached a settlement based on what was called the "no winners and no losers" formula. This revolution had turned violent, casting a shadow on society at large. The violence did not spare the students at all four Lebanese universities (the Jesuit St. Joseph University, American University of Beirut, the Lebanese University, and Arab University). Nor did it spare the students at the various colleges and advanced study centers affiliated with foreign universities. Each of these institutions had an independent student association, and each association had its own political orientation reflecting the sectarian loyalties prevalent in the environment from which the students came.

The Mathematical Sciences Center affiliate to the French Lyon University stood out for its religious and cultural diversity and the ways of its students, who, being science students, had a regard for critical thinking and objective, scientific approaches. It was there that I made new friends. Our discussions and analyses led us to conclude that as students, we had no role in the fate of what we sarcastically called "the great fateful issues" that were inciting debates and fighting and sapping the strength of student activists. We agreed that there was no point in our sophistic arguments over imagined or concocted past identities or romantic schemes that could be used to inflame futile political conflicts between parties or partisans with which we had no connection. We decided to focus our energies on "simple" issues that affected our present-day lives and tangibly shaped our future as students, individuals, and as a people in its patriotic, national, and humanitarian dimensions.

We were surprised when the silent majority of students at other universities spontaneously and enthusiastically adopted our proposals, which focused particularly on the provision of higher education laws; the development, reform, and improvement of the performance of educational institutions; the democratization of access to university education; and the protection of academic, cultural, and personal freedom. Our platform was met with a stunning response. With unexpected ease, it unified the ranks of the student movement in all the universities into the National Union of University Students. For the first time in the history of the student movement in Lebanon, the union included bodies representing students from different universities and colleges.

My fellow students gave me the honor of leading the student movement as the first president of the National Union of University Students. I also had the privilege of announcing the union's constitution and bylaws. My classmates and I would not have called for unifying student ranks around an enterprise of direct concern to us had we not been divested of our preconceptions, illusions, and tendency to judge others' intentions based on our assumptions about those intentions. This experience underscored how easily the young generation could abandon sectarian struggles and contentiousness when they have a unifying enterprise that is above personal and sectarian interests and they have leaders who are free of any sectarian ideology.

In 1962, Fuad Matni was elected president of the union as I left for France to continue my studies in engineering and economics, taking the advice of Father Lebret, the head of the mission of the Institute for Research, Training, Education, and Development. President of the Lebanese republic at the time, Fouad Chehab had tasked Lebret with formulating development plans to promote economic and social development and restructure the state, which was in decline. Father Lebret kindly advised me to continue my studies in areas that would qualify me for work in the Ministry of Planning, which then lacked personnel qualified in development planning.

In 1963, representatives of the students' elected bodies chose Nabih Berri to serve as the union president. It is noteworthy that the university students, after a sectarian-oriented revolution, entrusted the leadership of the student movement to Berri. His Excellency, now the Speaker of Parliament, would not have been elected president of the union at that time had sectarian ideology been fated to rule the minds of young people, and had Berri been considered a representative of the Shiite students in the union.

I returned from France with lofty dreams, fair academic baggage, and great admiration for French president Charles de Gaulle, who had rescued France from the humiliation of the June 1940 surrender. He saved his country from itself by ending its colonial adventure in Algeria in 1962 and then again from the overlapping previews of its constitutional institutions when he sought to create a Fifth Republic, confident in its history and supreme values.

When I returned from France, I joined the planning committee in the Ministry of Planning. I started my job with great enthusiasm, only to leave it less than a year later with great bitterness and frustration after the ministry had been transformed—shortly after President Chehab left—into a tool for legalizing the parceling out of the public domain to the sectarian leaders in the confessional system under the cover of development plans. I had to either resign or become a false witness for the confessional system. I had no opportunity to hesitate or dawdle in making the right decision. I resigned.

This brief experience at the beginning of my career helped me unmask the nature of our confessional system, which had been corrupted by its very genesis and operating mechanism. I became more certain that this system was the cause of corruption in the public administration and institutions, as well as civil society. I confirmed my belief that the confessional system is the main impediment to establishing national political parties, organizations, and entities, which could not develop under the sectarian system. This conviction led me to reject and oppose the system and work to undermine it.

The confessional system did not need an outside adversary to expose its defects, confirm its failure, or delegitimize it. Its leaders at the time did a much better job by exchanging insults, accusations, and court dates for lawsuits. The fragmentation of their ranks and dissolution of their institutions led to the signing of the ignominious 1969 Cairo Agreement between Lebanon and the PLO, which entrenched the ceding of Lebanon's sovereignty to Palestinian organizations. The debate over who signed, facilitated, inspired, and ratified the agreement no longer serves any purpose because the subservience of the ruling power and its lack of courage to exercise its sovereignty over Lebanon and protect its dignity led to its lack of ability to face its responsibilities. This ruling power will never have the capability to assume responsibility for our destiny.

The Cairo Agreement marked the end of Lebanon's independence. It entrenched the illegitimacy of our political system and paved the way for Syrian interference. Syria subjugated most of the confessional leaders and then took control of the tempo of the civil war raging among and within the religious communities.

But this Syrian interference was never able to extinguish the spark of freedom, decency, and critical thinking of the Lebanese elites, who confronted the schemes for elimination, containment, or dissolution with their scrawny arms and unbending will. The civil war finally brought the system to its inevitable end, pushing the sectarian leaders at the Taif conference to accept the abandonment of the confessional partitioning of power and agree to an alternative formula. The alternative formula was to be reached through national dialogue among the political, intellectual, and social elites within the civil society. It was supposed to preserve the Lebanese communities' differences, maintain pluralism, liberate Lebanon from its sectarian fetters, and prevent any one group from dominating another.

The Taif Agreement entrusted the president of the republic with conducting the national dialogue to devise an alternative nonsectarian system. This required renewing the search for the republic that we had lost in 1926. The renewed search ended abruptly after the assassination of President René Moawad. His successors lived in fear of a similar fate, which allowed for the resuscitation of the sectarian confessional system. His assassination also set back the dreams of those who had bet on the revival of the Lebanese republic as a laboratory of living together. Nevertheless, it confirmed that sectarianism could not win over the hearts and minds of the Lebanese.

In the spring of 2000, I published the book *The Other Lebanon*, in which I discuss the reasons that led to the failed state prior to the Taif Agreement. The book analyzes the causes for postponing the implementation of the Taif Agreement. It offers a vision for exiting the predicament and building a civil republic free of sectarian constraints and limits. The acknowledgment my book received by readers encouraged me to run for the parliamentary elections in the summer of 2000 in northern Lebanon's second district, which includes seventeen seats. I announced that I was running to create a platform for presenting my political reform program. My objective was to put abandonment of the sectarian system to a test of popular opinion. I called upon the voters to vote for my political program, not for me personally, and to choose their children's future rather than being solicitous for the future of the children of the professional political leaders.

My campaign rhetoric provoked the ire of more than one fellow candidate on the election list. My campaign slogan, "A Nation, Not An Exploitation," also angered the incumbent authority. They were not used to the idea of candidates talking with voters about political reform without falling back on partisanship and enticements. They did not relish the prospect of abandoning their traditional methods. Accordingly, they unashamedly and crudely resorted to influencing voters and warning them of the consequences of snubbing their directives. Moreover, they assiduously spread false rumors and openly meddled in voting.

I was completely surprised on Election Day. I thought I had woken some elitist circles to popular rejection of sectarianism, lining up behind leaders, and dependency to thereby affect their votes. Yet I was not expecting popular support, as indicated by the polling station results in various regions and among various religious communities and social segments. The results were apparently not expected by the incumbent powers as well, compelling the Ministry of Interior to refrain from announcing the election result for the seat for which I was running on the pretext of checking the results. The checking was staged in the absence of the candidates' representatives. The next day the interior minister announced that my opponent had won.

The election results—which I hoped would serve as a referendum on my nonsectarian political platform in a large, mixed area with multiple predilections and affiliations—convinced me that a broad number of the Lebanese public is opposed to the sectarian confessional system and would support a candidate who openly opposed it.

Starting in 2002, I was motivated to dedicate myself to formulate a social contract to which all Lebanese could adhere. The contract would be based on recognition of diversity and differences as well as equality and equal opportunity in a secular republic free of sectarian constraints or factional affiliations. I have worked with activists and colleagues in the democratic movement we have founded to launch a public campaign in north Lebanon to pave the way for a national democratic movement opposed to sectarianism and committed to the values pertaining to the secular republic.

In 2004 I published my book *The Road to the State*, which distills the ideas generated in hundreds of meetings that we held with colleagues to discuss a covenantal, civil state—a state that could unleash the creative energies of the Lebanese to achieve the economic and cultural miracle we deserve. *The Road to the State* presents my ideas about the dependable national dialogue and was launched that same year. We imagined that the time had come to leave behind the sectarian confessional system and move on to the alternative system. But the assassination of Prime Minister Rafic Hariri on February 14, 2005, sent us reeling back to square one, unleashing panic and fear of "the other."

Sectarian convulsions were instigated from multiple quarters. Proponents of a state based on citizenship rather than religious communities found less and less ground on which to take a stand as their enemies and false claimants closed ranks to expropriate that ground.

The parliamentary elections of 2005 saw the return of panic-stricken religious communities. They redistributed the country and dismantled divisions, pushing citizens into the impasse of religious communities. The sectarian advocates returned to indiscriminately and shamelessly ravage the memory and marginalize "the other."

I was appalled by the sectarian alignments spawned by the horrifying assassination and had never felt so alienated. I believed that our society, which had suffered from an illegitimate domination and subjugation, was no longer able to cope with the anxieties engendered by the sectarian ideology and its possession of our minds and wills.

In the introduction to my book *The Parliament of Tomorrow*, published soon after the elections, I related:

> Early in the morning on Election Day, I went to Tripoli, a city that is a part of me. I loved its poor and toiling classes, its intellectuals, and its

leading personalities, who received me as a guest in their homes, forums, and associations. On that wretched day I looked for all of them. I called on them one by one yet did not find them. I was met with silence. I found only the raging sectarian spaniel foaming and frothing at the mouth, unleashed in the open. I recalled my friend and schoolmate Nazir al-Hossami. I wanted to tug on his hand and pull him next to me. Maybe together we could stand up to the bulls charging us, each in turn. Would he remember that the homeland equally belongs to all of us?

In the wake of Election Day, which saw sectarian discord and the revival of murderous passions that denied the right of others to exist, I lost the certainty that had inspired me to write *The Road to the State*. I imagined that the tribes and sects had resumed competing over and snapping at the limbs of the pure and rational Lebanese Democratic Movement. I made the only objective choice available to me on that day: I announced I would not engage in any electoral activity now or in the future. I distanced myself from the alignments that had led to the ruin of what remained of political life and the quasi state. I returned to the profession I had mastered, the profession I had loved and practiced since 1966. I went back to the BUTEC engineering firm that I had founded. BUTEC had become one of the most important contracting companies in the Arab world and another testament to the Lebanese individual and the moral fiber and nobility of thousands of young Lebanese men and women who have worked with me and given me the strength and determination to again be optimistic.

For me, optimism may be an incurable disease or addiction. I regained my optimism after I resumed my career and had the chance to carefully review the sectarian situation in our society. I regained my positive outlook from the clarity of thought of tens of thousands of Lebanese engineers, technicians, managers, and laborers who continued working together even in the darkest of times. I was grateful to realize that over the past fifty years of our company's existence, we had not had a single incident, complaint, grievance, or accusation related to religious affiliation or difference.

The overwhelming majority of private sector companies and their production facilities are nonsectarian in their orientations, practices, and hiring, meaning our people are still nonsectarian at heart. The achievements of individual initiative in the private sector can be duplicated in the state institutions and in administrations that have been usurped by religious communities. However, this can happen only if public servants can be freed from the subjugation of the sectarian leaders who have divided up the public domain among themselves.

By contrast, I am alarmed by the persistent migration of young Lebanese during the past few years, and of promising private enterprises, which maintained their faith in Lebanon under the harshest conditions. These companies have transferred what they have earned through their hard work and activity throughout the world to their homeland, providing for the possibility of closing Lebanon's balance of payment and budget deficit, which have accumulated through usurpation and corruption.

Private initiative, with its toughness, resolve, and genius, embodies the honor of Lebanon and its people's nobility and promise to civilization. However, private initiative has begun to face ingratitude, false accusations, and denial of its role, not only from the professional political establishment but from the parties that claim to oppose the failed sectarian confessional system. A query is being raised in earnest about the background of the oppressive campaign against the private sector, which rescued what remained of this country; the attempt to demonize it; and the role of the sectarian political establishment in targeting the civil, nonsectarian private sector. We believe the private sector remains the last obstacle to the complete appropriation by sectarian leaders of public utilities, the land, and the scenery. The campaign against the private sector is conclusive evidence of the corruption of the sectarian ideology and the system it has spawned.

I am deeply worried about the repercussions of Lebanese companies relocating abroad. This process is divesting the economic environment of its promising elements, leaving behind middlemen, unprincipled people, and plundered state institutions. It could ultimately bankrupt Lebanon, dragging it into the violence that always erupts when economic growth stalls.

My determination to struggle to reclaim the secular, democratic republic for the Lebanese people, who have been able to preserve their unique characteristics despite the harshness and bitterness they have endured, compelled me to make my choice and write a letter to my colleagues at BUTEC. I informed them that on December 31, 2014, I was stepping down as chairman of the board of BUTEC Group to rededicate my means to national action on the expectation that I could hopefully help achieve a small part of our aspirations. I explained my motives in the letter as follows:

> I would never have abandoned the profession in which I have become proficient had I been able to resist the impulse to dedicate the remaining part of my life to our country. I now feel certain that it is facing an existential threat to its survival, and it no longer is permissible for anyone to shirk his duty. I have decided to do what I believe to be my national and humanitarian duty. Starting today, I will dedicate all my resolve and willpower to gathering the fragments of our torn society and invigorating its life forces.

Thus, in early 2015 I left my career and started searching anew for my republic. I have searched for it in our modern history; in our ancient heritage; in the ideas of the nineteenth-century Arab Renaissance; in the endeavors of our Founding Fathers; in our social movements; in our uprisings, revolutions, and setbacks; in our experiments in living together; and in the unique attributes of the Lebanese people, which have been shaped by bonds of daily life and by shared religious, cultural, and civilizational content.

I went back to the beginning, to the republic locomotive, which had embarked in the wrong direction in 1926 and is still lost, imprisoned in the crowded cell of the confessional leaders in an archaic sectarian trap. I returned to the departure station to search of a road map providing directions to a fair, clear social contract for the Lebanese, a contract I believe is necessary to put the train back on course and stop it from going down the wrong track again, toward the prison of sectarian confessionalism.

I am certain we will not find this social contract in a book, nor will it be generated in a conference or by decree of a ruler or arbitrator. This contract between the people of Lebanon will be concluded only by the Lebanese. It is endorsed by the dialogue between intellectual, social, and political elites which the president of the republic must nurture under the Taif Agreement and Article 95 of the constitution. Our president should be a statesperson and visionary; who is proud, virtuous, and confident in himself or herself and his or her people; who keeps promises and upholds charters; and who has the stature to lead the national dialogue and complete implementing the Taif Agreement to redirect the journey of the republic onto the right track. Thus, we shall not lose our way again and return to war, and our country, the country our people deserve, will not be bereft of its spirit, culture, and freedom.

This book offers a vision that many share with me for reclaiming the republic through political reform, social and economic renaissance, and promotion of freedom and culture.

Part I

A ROAD MAP FOR POLITICAL REFORM: IMPLEMENTING THE TAIF AGREEMENT

Introduction

The day after General Michel Suleiman was elected president of Lebanon, I wrote him an open letter that was published in the Lebanese newspaper *An-Nahar* on May 31, 2008. The letter posed a number of questions that had beset the Lebanese since the Syrian withdrawal from Lebanon in 2005. I sent the letter against the backdrop of Suleiman's unwillingness, before he was elected, to reveal his vision for how he would discharge his constitutional role to fully implement the Taif Agreement and revive efforts to have a state with unified authority.

Despite the circumstances surrounding his election, the Lebanese saw it as a possible light at the end of the tunnel. With the encouragement of friends, I decided to engage him in an exchange on our vision of the president's role in leading the floundering ship of state to safe shores. I did not want the letter to anger him. I had hoped he would succeed in discharging his presidential role, as hoped by the Lebanese during that difficult time.

However, Suleiman finished his term in 2014, leaving behind a vacuum as the election of a new president had by then become a rather difficult, complicated venture, owing to the ossification of the political system and complexities of discharging constitutional responsibilities. It may be useful here to cite the content of this open letter:

Your Excellency, Mr. President,

Today is another day. You have become the president. You will either be the most eminent president in Lebanon's history or the last president of a country whose will to survive has been sapped by compromises and bargains.

They placed you at the apex of a decrepit system of government that has become ossified. Its ruling power has become a council of religious stakeholders and tribal notables, with a divided authority; and a state split into statelets and fiefdoms that quarrel over land, sovereignty, and religion.

Time will not be on your side. With each passing day, your window of opportunity becomes narrower. If you are deemed weak, you will be devoured. You are in a race against time to overcome the vacuum and paralysis facing you, before you are overcome by time.

From where should you begin?

Begin from where your predecessor, President Fouad Chehab, left off, from that bitter truth that confronted him, which he declared in his famous letter of resignation that there is no way to stabilize, sustain, and develop a state under a sectarian confessional system.

It is your duty to start by implementing the Taif Agreement and the Constitution. Are you not the trustee of the Constitution? The Taif Agreement's most important provision is its affirmation that abandonment of the sectarian system is a national goal that must be achieved.

The pact in the Taif requires the president of the republic to head a dialogue committee tasked with exploring an alternative to the confessional system—an alternative that highlights coexistence and the achievement of equality and fairness among Lebanese without sectarian constraints and paves the way for building an accomplished modern state that nurtures its people and is faithful to its covenants and precepts.

You will issue the decree of the first-term government. The cabinet statement should be limited to one key paragraph, which dispenses with the need for any other statement, namely the commitment of the government to implement the provisions of the Taif Agreement in letter and spirit and to form a national dialogue committee to design a system to replace our confessional system. The dialogue commission should comprise the legitimate representatives of Lebanese society from among the intellectual, moral, and cultural personalities who desire to formulate a renewed covenant that regulates our national life.

Needless to say, there is no chance of building an integrated state that takes care of its citizens and nurtures their role, nor is there any chance that such a state will enjoy stability or continuity, unless that state is based on a written, binding, permanent charter that affirms national precepts and courageously and fairly defines the identity of the state that we seek, including its values and the principles that govern and protect the freedom of individuals and preserve the rights of groups.

Can the dialogue committee provided in Article 95 of the Constitution produce a social contract to which the Lebanese agree, one that entrenches the foundations of a peaceful living together and equality among all citizens and affirms ways for preserving the unique features and rights of the various religious communities and groups while protecting individual freedoms?

Every great enterprise starts with a small dream. It is not a luxury to dream of a modern, democratic, civil state; a state of abundance, prosperity, justice, and humane values. It is not a luxury to dream of a Lebanon with a resplendent culture, that is a laboratory for the meeting of civilizations and a model of balanced pluralism and security in which no one seeks to negate anyone and no one group dominates another.

Mr. President, for our dream to be realized, we have no desire for you to be a consensual president, a temporary savior, chieftain, crisis manager or overseer of a durable or quickly broken truce. It is your fate to be the president and to confront our destiny by presenting a national project we can rally around and implement to resurrect the Lebanon we seek. If we unfortunately see that you are not resolved, it would be better for you to resign, as Fouad Chehab did, so that it will not someday be said that you came simply to bear witness and then departed. History does not forget.

I hope President Suleiman would not be the last president of the republic. I hope the elected president would declare his platform, identity, and convictions—particularly his conviction of the need to uphold his constitutional oath and finish implementing the Taif Agreement.

The reason I shake off the dust from my letter to the former president of the republic is to help underscore two key points. First, the road map for political reform can be found in the Taif Agreement. Second, continued avoidance of the full implementation of this agreement exacerbates sectarian sentiment and merely kicks the problem down the road, allowing for an inglorious escape into a future where the problem will persist.

Chatine, the author's village and birthplace

The author's renovated traditional Lebanese house in Batroun

The author heading National Union of University Students in 1961

The author during the year 2000 parliamentary elections

Chapter 1

THE LEGITIMACY AND PERMANENCE OF THE LEBANESE STATE

The fierce debates in the twentieth century over whether Lebanon is a legitimate and viable nation have abated after having greatly stoked fears and factional divisiveness and thwarted attempts to reform the system and free it from the scourge of confessionalism. The geopolitical developments that have swept the Arab world have helped temper overenthusiastic, uncalculated schemes to unify the Arab world. Today, Lebanon is indisputably unique in the Arab world for having evolved as the result of a conscious popular will, even if that will has not been ubiquitous at the time.

To a certain degree, the Lebanese—and international public opinion—firmly believe the success of the Lebanese experiment of living together is vital to the survival of human civilization whose core values are now under threat. They believe the preservation of this experiment is no more a burden on the international community as it has become a fundamental requirement for promoting the philosophy of coexistence—or better said, living together—in a world that has become a mixed global village. It is no longer possible for any ethnicity, religion, or race to exist in isolation.

Thus, Lebanon's mission and the responsibility of its intellectual and political elite transcend Lebanon to encompass humanity in general. It is essential that the Lebanese experiment succeed. The country must transition from the romantic, demagogic approaches and come to an understanding of its raison d'etre and the basic postulates and norms of living together, which were adopted by the Lebanese constituencies as a covenant for establishing a nurturing state.

Three points to consider include

1. the genesis and continuity of states;
2. respect for covenants is a condition for the survival of pluralistic states; and
3. the hierarchy of juridical norms.

1. The Genesis and Continuity of States

The state is an abstract concept. It reflects the will of the inhabitants of a land to live together within a political entity. It embodies the desire of the groups comprising a society to join in a national, unified community based on a collective memory to implement a jointly conceived national project that fairly allocates resources and gives everyone an equal chance.

The desire of living together is the cornerstone of the genesis and stability of a state and the source of its legitimacy. The state does not truly exist per se. It is not a fixed, eternal reality. The state's stability and sustainability depend on the desire of its constituencies to live together. Thus, the state can no longer be conflated with the nation in a single political concept. In fact, the state is an overarching structure that regulates the lives of the constituencies who belong to a nation. These constituencies depend on the state to provide for prosperity, security, decent life, and protection of their rights to equality and respect for their respective features.

Making a distinction between the nation and the state serves to emphasize that the problem does not lie in the Lebanese nation. In Lebanon all societal segments share a sense of patriotism and a desire to belong to the nation, even if they sometimes differ in their expression of this desire. They all equally suffer from the state's failure to manage society and transform it into a modern, civil society that is united behind an overarching plan for the future as an alternative to a society that remains divided into factions led by a regressive sectarian ideology.

While the desire for living together underlies the genesis of a state, it alone does not suffice to establish a stable state capable of dealing with major crises. A state cannot continue as a legitimate entity unless it protects its citizens' right to justice and equality to thereby preclude any one group from feeling wronged, deprived, or frustrated. Each sectarian group in Lebanese society believes, rightly so, that its rights are enshrined in the nation and that its partnership in the nation is predicated on the protection of those rights.

The desire of living together is natural in a country that is ethnically homogeneous or is a social and cultural melting pot. However, this is not the case in pluralistic states, where this desire must be backed by covenants that serve as recognized legal norms for deciding issues or conflicts arising from diverging purposes and group interests. Such covenants are tantamount to a legal shield. Adhering to them prevents doubt, fear, and wariness of "the other" from taking hold.

2. Respect for Covenants Is a Condition for the Survival of Pluralistic States

A covenant on living together does not arise from a vacuum. Rather, it results from the convergence of desires or interests of the groups comprising society and is based on the conditions that they accept as a basis for their participation in a common nation.

Lebanon did not have a written, permanent founding covenant. However, it would not have survived had its evolution not been regulated by conventions and traditions that have become axioms or precepts. They may have been assailed by the Lebanese themselves, but they have continued to serve as a suitable agreed-upon convention for deciding many conflictual matters. Ultimately, the Taif Agreement was concluded to affirm and renew such precepts. The agreed social contract paves the way for enshrining its provisions in a fair, clear, and permanent contract. It ends the floundering of the country amid a multiplicity of interpretations. It relieves the nation of its cumbersome system of compromises, haggling, and indecision. Finally, it plots the course for building an accomplished modern civil state free of division or segregation.

Lebanese groups have implicitly or explicitly agreed to coexist as a nation since the Lebanese entity first emerged based on mutual understandings and customs that have become precepts and binding agreements, the most important of which are as follows:

An Implicit Founding Contract after the Incidents of 1860

Lebanon was dragged into the international competition over the disintegrating Ottoman Empire in the nineteenth century, which led to tragic intercommunal incidents in 1860. Thereafter, the Lebanese returned to their traditions and mutual culture of tolerance and solidarity of prior eras, expressing their continued desire of living together based on a formula that provided for the shared bearing of responsibilities. These traditions led to a historical settlement in the form of the Mount Lebanon Mutasarrifate province protocol (the Beyoglu Protocol), which provided for sectarian power sharing—without reliance on a census—in the Administrative Council of Mount Lebanon and for sectarian quotas with respect to the administration of the Mutasarrifate. The ruler of Mount Lebanon was a mutasarrif (designated by the Ottomans a mutasarrif was an administrative authority who was appointed directly by the sultan) and unobjected by the other five powers (France, England, Austria, Prussia, and Italy).

The Conventions Observed during the Mandate Period

The declaration of the State of Greater Lebanon in 1920 culminated the efforts of the Maronite patriarch Elias Hoayek, who had been commissioned for this task by most of the representatives of the Lebanese communities. The day after the declaration, the desire for living together was reaffirmed not only by the Maronite Church (the Maronite Church in Lebanon is the largest Christian denomination in the country) in accordance with its historical precepts but by most of the other communities. A virtually unanimous national consensus added the last link when the National Pact (*al-Mithaq al-Watani*, an unwritten agreement, which came into being in the summer of 1943 as a result of numerous meetings between Bechara el-Khoury [a Maronite Christian], Lebanon's first president after independence, and the first prime minister, Riyad el-Solh [a Sunni Muslim] was declared.

The French Mandate maintained the procedural formula for living together based on the rule of sectarian division that had been followed since Ottoman Mutasarrifate times. This state of affairs was considered temporary. It was intended to avoid breaching prevailing conventions, the violation of which required a national consensus. It is worth mentioning that the division of responsibilities among the groups under the Ottoman

Mutasarrifate system occurred with the consent of the groups themselves. It was based on the representation of all communities and did not adhere to specific numbers or percentages. This method of sectarian representation, which did not involve a census, continued in the French Mandate period.

The 1943 National Pact on the Eve of the Declaration of Lebanese Independence

The National Pact was ratified unanimously in 1943 to avoid aggravating the fears and doubts that were bubbling over in that troubled period. The Pact was declared in a communiqué issued by the first government headed by Riyad el-Solh. It represented the outcome of the mutual understandings which he reached with President Bechara el-Khoury each acting on behalf of the Muslim and Christian communities respectively. An unparalleled national consensus enshrined these mutual understandings in a pact that was binding on all Lebanese. These understandings became the foundation for the Pact of the Lebanese regarding their nation's independence and permanence. The 1943 National Pact included the following mutual commitments made by the Lebanese groups:

- Lebanon is not the country of Christians or of Muslims exclusively. It is the country for the living together of both communities, which entails equal participation in governance and decision making.
- The Christians concede any demand for foreign protection, while the Muslims accept the Lebanese state within its current borders as a permanent, independent, sovereign entity whose policies emanate from its government. The government's decisions are based on the supreme interests of the Lebanese people.
- Lebanon is part of the Arab family and will not grant imperialist powers safe passage or a foothold to act against

its Arab brethren. Lebanon is in complete solidarity with the Arab interest and avoids involvement in the policies of axes that could cause dissension among Arab countries.

The National Pact affirmed the historical Muslim-Christian Pact over Lebanon's future as an independent sovereign nation, whose policies are inspired by its people's supreme interests. Preempting future difficulties, it also affirmed Lebanon's neutrality and refusal to enter the game of regional and international axes, as if the historical leadership at that time had advance warning of the danger that the sectarian groups would be drawn into foreign loyalties that would plunge them into the conflicts of others.

The more these commitments were upheld in the government's domestic and foreign policies in the period following the Pact, the more Lebanon enjoyed calm and prosperity. On the other hand, the more these commitments were shaken by regional and international dissension, the more national unity was torn asunder, providing an opening for chaos and civil strife as happened in 1958 and 1975 and as is happening today.

The Taif Agreement (National Reconciliation Charter) Ending the Civil War

The National Reconciliation Charter covered the main disputed issues underlying the civil wars, disturbances, and foreign interventions. It also covered procedural matters concerning the functioning of the political institutions and cooperation and balance among them. It thus sought to reconcile the requirements of the post–civil war transitional period with the precepts of the desired historical settlement. The Lebanese themselves were subsequently charged with holding a dialogue to formulate these precepts away from the influence of regional conflicts.

Lebanese society welcomed the provisions of the charter approved in Taif. They believed adherence to these provisions would ultimately completely resolve the issues over clashes in the past that had led to wars and conflicts. These provisions were included in the National Reconciliation Accord and in the preamble to the Constitution known as the Taif Constitution, which is simply the Lebanese Constitution of 1926 as amended through 1990.

Preamble to the Constitution

Following are the provisions of the Taif Agreement that are included in the preamble to the Constitution that have become precepts that may neither be disregarded nor violated:

a. Lebanon is a sovereign, free, independent country. It is the definitive homeland for all its citizens. It is unified in its territory, people, and institutions within the boundaries that are stipulated in its constitution and recognized internationally.

b. Lebanon is Arab in its identity and affiliation. It is an active founding member of the League of Arab States and abides by its conventions. Lebanon is also an active founding member of the United Nations and abides by its conventions and by the Universal Declaration of Human Rights. The government incorporates the principles of such conventions in all fields and areas without exception.

c. Lebanon is a parliamentary democratic republic that is based on respect for general freedoms, foremost of which are the freedom of opinion and belief. It is also based on social justice, and equality of rights and duties among all citizens without discrimination or preference.

d. The people are the source of authorities and sovereignty, which they shall exercise through the constitutional institutions.

e. The political system is based on the separation, balancing, and cooperation of powers.

f. The economic system is liberal and guarantees private initiative and private ownership.

g. Balanced development—regional, educational, social, and economic—is a basic pillar of the unity of the state and the stability of the government.

h. The abolition of the confessional political system is a fundamental national goal that must be achieved according to a staged plan.

i. Lebanese territory is one for all Lebanese. Every Lebanese is entitled to live in any part thereof and to enjoy the rule of law. There shall be no segregation of the people on the basis of any type of belonging, and no fragmentation, partition, or settlement of non-Lebanese in Lebanon.

j. Any authority which contradicts the precepts of living together shall be illegal.

To eliminate any confusion, we should note here that confessionalism (i.e., the apportionment of political power and the public realm among religious communities—a system known as the sectarian apportionment system) has never at any time been agreed upon among Lebanese as a condition of their living together.

On the contrary, the Lebanese have always deemed the confessional system to be a temporary procedural formula that must be replaced with another formula. Obviously, if the confessional system had been provided in a national pact, the Taif conferees would not have been permitted to abandon it.

The Taif conferees approved a pact that affirms the oneness of citizenship and the full equality of citizens and communities as the fundamental base for rebuilding the state. However, the single most important provision of the Taif Agreement is its stipulation of the need to move beyond the existing sectarian confessional system, which was the main reason why living together has floundered and civil strife and destructive wars have erupted.

The Taif Agreement affirms that the surest path to the establishment of an alternative to the condemnable confessional system is a national dialogue among the Lebanese themselves, led by the president of the republic. The agreement set the date for the start of the dialogue on the day after the formation of the first parliament elected based on parity between Christian and Muslim Lebanese, which occurred in 1992.

The president of the republic was assigned as head of the Dialogue Commission under the constitution and should have launched the dialogue in 1992. As a consequence of the assassination of President Moawad in 1990, neither President Elias Hrawi nor any of his successors, for well-known reasons, wanted to fulfill their oath by boldly embarking on this rescue mission. The implementation of the Taif Agreement and the constitutional reforms have thus remained frozen, giving new life to the confessional system, which has become more rooted in people's minds and more destructive of what is left of the Lebanese state.

Regional conflicts have led sectarian leaders to exploit domestic tensions in order to espouse political rhetoric that defends the sectarian confessional system and justifies renouncement of the Taif Agreement. The most dangerous aspect of such rhetoric is that it confuses the agreement with the constitution; it confuses the end with the means and the permanent with the temporary. Such rhetoric seeks to exacerbate the fears of the demoralized Lebanese groups in order to exploit those fears as a shield for the archaic sectarian confessional system—the very system that has destroyed civil peace and threatened pluralism—and thwart the Lebanese dream of freedom, culture, and development.

Unfortunately, most of the religious parties in Lebanon tend to use the Taif Agreement for sectarian purposes. This leads them to depart from the essence of the agreement/charter that the Taif conferees approved to end a tragedy that nearly wiped out the basis of our national existence. The contractual, binding nature of the Taif Agreement is uncontested even though the procedural provisions of the post–Taif Constitution cannot be construed as a charter or covenant. It is thus wrong to maintain that these provisions cannot be corrected, amended, or supplemented, as if they were immutable.

3. Hierarchy of Juridical Norms

There is widespread confusion and a near universal belief in political and media circles that every provision in the Lebanese Constitution, which is known as the Taif Constitution, is a binding covenant not subject to amendment. This confusion stems from the blurring between a constitution and a covenant in the minds of the Lebanese public, who do not distinguish between their corresponding legal effects or are unaware of the hierarchy of juridical norms.

It has become axiomatic that the *natural rights* of *individuals* and *groups* have absolute priority over all other rights, including the contractual obligations enshrined in an agreed-upon charter. The reason is that natural rights derive their legitimacy from the premises of *public order;* public order in turn is based on rules and principles society deems authoritative. Recourse to such rules and values is the fundamental framework to regulate relations among the entities that play a role in protecting and nurturing society. The essential values enshrined in the democratic system, which are accepted by the Lebanese as a basis for their living together and the formation of the governing authorities, are the right to equality, justice, freedom of belief and thought, legitimate parliamentary representation, and the rotation of power. These precepts have precedence over any covenant, constitution, or laws.

Second in the hierarchy of legal norms are covenants that the partners in the nation have concluded expressly or implicitly and which they regard as the basis for their partnership. Such agreements are concluded when a joint partnership is established or as a result of understandings for resolving chronic crises facing the partners. The contractual provisions in the Taif Agreement that address the core disputed issues that have led to tragedies in the past have become a covenant that is binding on all Lebanese in all matters that do not conflict with public order precepts.

Third in the hierarchy of legal norms is the Constitution, the basis of the functioning of any political system. The Constitution engineers and regulates the rhythm and performance of the political system. Thus, except for the covenantal provisions that comprise the public order precepts, the provisions of the Constitution are adjusted according to the state's changing requirements for implementing its political, developmental, social, and cultural plans. So whereas provisions of the Constitution cannot contradict public order and the covenantal contract, they should not remain frozen and entrenched such that their defects and ambiguities would be disregarded and exploited to justify the decommissioning of constitutional institutions.

Positive laws passed by the legislative institutions are fourth in the hierarchy of juridical norms. Such laws must comply with constitutional provisions and must not conflict with covenants or public order. Ignoring or denying these principles corrupts or nullifies the law, breaches order, exacerbates the fears of sectarian groups, and unleashes sectarian schemes.

Chapter 2

BASIC PRECEPTS FOR THE DIALOGUE

In this period of acute sectarian and religious conflict, and divisive factional schemes spreading throughout the Arab world, a call for an objective and rational dialogue among the Lebanese to complete implementing the Taif Agreement might sound dissonant and beyond the logic of current times. In reality, the Lebanese need to come together more now than ever in order to hold a dialogue to preserve their culture of living together and to ensure the success of the civilized world's gamble on our unique experiment. Now more than ever, civilization, whose basic values are under threat, needs to witness a successful experience of living together as an example of hope.

Our only chance of salvation is through a constructive national dialogue. Such a dialogue has no chance of success unless it is based on covenantal precepts already approved as a basis for formulating an alternative political system to the confessional system, which all groups agree must be abandoned. Following are the basic precepts.

1. Understanding the Cause of Lebanon's Chronic Unrest and Crises

It is no more useful to simply curse fate and stand by powerlessly, as our crises intensify and as religious communities and tribes and their partisans line up to trade accusations or blame our marginalized people or absentee civil society, or simply blame our misfortune to have been born at this despairing time in the history of our stricken country.

We must first acknowledge that the crises are not inevitable. Rather, they undoubtedly stem from a political system whose composition and dynamics of functioning must lead to corruption and flabbiness in the state structure, to fragmentation of society, and an atrophied sense of citizenship. Despite the consensus to abandon the confessional system, our people lack the courage to envision the future that we can create as an alternative to a past that was imposed on us and leads us continually toward national suicide.

Politics, defined as "the art of administering cities," addresses all aspects of life, whether social, economic, or cultural. It also addresses civil peace and societal security. The ability of constitutional institutions to provide economic and social growth, security, and prosperity for all citizens depends on the nature of the political system. The success or failure of political initiative depends primarily on the political system's ability to govern. It must be able to limit conflicting interests and other conflicts. It must create harmony among the various concerned parties to ensure that they function in an integrated manner.

The state is an institutional entity that embodies the regulatory, legal, and logistical structures needed to manage public affairs. To perform its duties well, the state must have oneness in addition to being hierarchical and be neutral toward its citizens in managing the conflicting interests of groups and individuals. The state alone must be entitled to monopolize the exercise of legitimate violence needed to apply its laws and to ensure its citizens' security.

This is the definition of the state in political science. Does the state that we have correspond to the definition of an establishment capable of realizing our destinies? Clearly, the council of religious communities that we call the state does not meet any of the above-mentioned criteria; it is a strange, disjointed creation with at least three heads. It is not hierarchical but rather a mix of overlapping and intermeshing authorities distributed among feudal groups that champion one or another religious community. Each religious community is embodied by its leader. The institutions of the state are not neutral. Each is unashamedly dedicated to serving its head for his or her personal benefit or the benefit of the group to which he or she belongs. Our state comprises statelets that quarrel with each other over sovereignty, legitimacy, and decision making and engage in illegal violence to achieve their factional objectives. The simple conclusion dictated by logic is that what we call the state is nothing but a backward tribal entity comprised of religious communities, tribes, families, and financial or economic interests.

To avoid blaming ourselves and put an end to frustrated lamenting over our misfortune, we must acknowledge that our misfortune is generated by a booby-trapped, reform-resistant system framework.

2. The Confessional System Hinders the Emergence of a Viable State

The Lebanese system is based on dividing the public domain among religious communities. It has been part of our national life for the past one hundred and fifty years. Confessionalism, at its origin, has been morally justified as preventing the exclusion or deprivation of any religious community within the system. However, this objective has not been achieved; the opposite has occurred. In practice, confessionalism has cemented the overlap between factional interests and the public interest. This is due to the natural propensity of the sectarian representatives, who have agreed to this division of power and resources, to engage in conflicts and struggles over the size of their shares. This game is reflected in the balance of power among religious communities. It has legitimized the instrumentalization of religion in power struggles between and within religious communities. The ultimate result has been the emergence of vertical divisions between groups and the exacerbation of partisan contradictions between religious communities as an alternative to political competition over projects that contribute to the development of society.

Under the confessional system, the public domain is apportioned by religious communities according to quotas. A civil servant holding a particular position will naturally seek to fortify his or her hold on that position. For this purpose, he or she will tend to stir up sectarian sentiment to mobilize his or her sect, fabricating causes for alarm and polarization. Ultimately, the government loses its unity, chain of command, neutrality, legitimacy, and cohesion. The state is then bereft of an authority that can interpose itself to resolve conflicts of interests and conflicts between groups. Then, a foreign authority is brought in to arbitrate, and it becomes the actual ruler of the country in a position to engage in a power game, bullying the concerned parties into subservience, and transforming the country into an arena for settling the conflicts of others.

The apportionment or quota system has also caused our sense of citizenship to atrophy by setting up religious communities as intermediaries in all temporal affairs between citizens and the state. Humans crave a sense of belonging. This is a psychological need in addition to being a biological one. Humans will easily incline toward the ties offered by groups sharing similar features (religious, tribal, ethnic) if they are not provided with a unifying bond consisting of a modern state's cultural and humanitarian values and societal undertakings. French philosopher Henri

Bergson argues that mentally based affiliations—such as national affiliation with a patron state, human civilization, or cultural identity—better attract the loyalty of individuals than primary, instinctive ones. However, we must acknowledge that our political system, which is unable to offer a viable national project and which attracts the enthusiasm of individuals and meets their expectations and ambitions is responsible for the situation where loyalty to the sect is given precedence over loyalty to a failed state. Accordingly, the individual Lebanese is rendered a member of a congregation rather than a citizen of a state.

This system lacks accountability. It has destroyed our political life, transforming it into a clash between communities or a tribal clash. It is also responsible for our crisis-ridden economy, our derelict security, and the frightening emigration of our youth, which is emptying our country of its life force. Most importantly, the system itself is to blame for our sectarian groups having loyalty to foreign countries.

The overwhelming majority of the Lebanese people are convinced that the confessional system in our country—despite its proclaimed justifications and problematic discourse—is intrinsically corrupt, is deficient in its performance, and will inevitably lead to an ineffective, corrupt, failed state.

3. The Failure of Civil Society

There is a consensus among the Lebanese to blame the ineffectiveness and failure on the political leadership that has been ruling since independence. Yet the intellectual elite tend to place some of this blame on Lebanese civil society because it reelects parliamentary representatives from the same political class whose practices have been the brunt of the electorates' complaints. Nevertheless, they assert that the chronic crisis of our deficient system deprives civil society of its immune system, rendering it vulnerable to the spread of contagious problems in our neighborhood and to conceding its role to sectarian and family groupings.

The assertion that the political class is to blame for what we are suffering finds, in many circles, a sympathetic response, albeit one constrained by reality. For it must be obvious that substituting one politician or member of Parliament for another has not cured the malady. In such cases, the newcomer is obliged to submit to the confessional system and follow its entrenched behavior. Otherwise, he or she becomes embittered and leaves unceremoniously. In most cases he or she fails to make any changes while he himself or she herself is changed by the system.

At the same time, some are quick to absolve the confessional apportionment system of responsibility for the government's paralysis and weakness. They blame Lebanese civil society for having produced the political class that has gotten us into this tragic situation. This conclusion confuses cause and effect, deepens the sense of frustration and fear of change, and entrenches the belief that the Lebanese and their politicians are unable to govern themselves. It leads to an ideology of impasse and resignation, causing position holders to behave like a defeated army whose members have scattered.

Thus the problem is not due to civil society, which the confessional system has paralyzed and put out of action. Citizenship cannot take shape as a political reality until the state truly takes shape. The Lebanese sense of loyalty to the nation will remain based on fickle emotions until citizens believe the state is politically unified and provides an alternative to factional arrangements. The theory that society is to blame is a weapon in the hands of its opponents, who use it to distract from the real cause of the problem and to avoid dealing with political reforms that can restore the health and cohesion of the state and society.

The consensus is that the Lebanese people are distinct and tolerant, since if not for their abilities there would have been no Lebanon under our flawed system and peculiar balance of power.

The lack of a well-established, just, impartial state enterprise able to unify its citizens is causing the breakup of our civil society into family and sectarian groups, rooted in the past.

This dilemma resulted from the inability to create an alternative system that can spare the individual from the indecision he or she feels in his or her sense of belonging to his or her family and sectarian group on the one hand and his or her desire to be a citizen in a state that he or she respects and that respects him or her on the other hand. It is unacceptable to place the blame on society in order to absolve the confessional apportionment system and justify our renouncement of the Taif Agreement's fundamental stipulation of the abandonment of this system.

4. The Lebanese State Neutrality Is a Covenantal Obligation

The Lebanese state, upon which we depend to provide the prerequisites of stability for our country, would not have gained independence or been able to continue if not for the 1943 National Pact, which embodies a covenantal settlement between Christian and Muslim Lebanese. It was adopted to reconcile between groups with differing goals and aspirations based on a mutual commitment and adherence to fixed principles and precepts as a basic condition for the continuation of the national partnership and unity.

This pact confirms the state's unity, oneness of national affiliation, and avoidance of regional fights and struggles. It includes a provision enshrining Lebanon's neutrality. Bassem el-Jisr in his book *The 1943 Pact*, quotes the text of the Pact, which was written by the historian Yusuf Ibrahim Yazbeck and reviewed by President Bechara el-Khoury who confirmed the Pact's precise meaning in his memoirs. Following is the third paragraph of the Pact:

> Lebanon is part of the Arab family and a founding member of the Arab League. It will not grant

imperialist powers safe passage or a foothold to act against its Arab brethren. Lebanon is in complete solidarity with the Arab interest and shall avoid involvement in the policies of axes that could cause dissension among the Arab countries.

The National Pact established Lebanon's independence. Its three paragraphs are related to general principles and cover the precepts and mutual understandings observed by the Lebanese. It affirms their desire for equality and living together, acknowledges their pluralistic society, and commits to avoidance of dissension and conflicts that could sweep the Arab world to thereby preserve the unity and solidarity of the Lebanese. It affirms that their loyalty to living together takes precedence over any other loyalty. In this regard, we note the following:

- None of the Lebanese groups, even in their darkest times, have renounced the first article of the Pact, which expresses the desire of the Lebanese to live together equally.
- Neither Christian nor Muslim Lebanese have publicly reneged on their commitment to abandon foreign protection in lieu of the recognition of each of the communities of the permanence and sovereignty of the Lebanese nation, as provided in the second article of the Pact (although every party uses this article for its own purposes to take the other party severely to task for its intentions).
- The third article of the National Pact, which expresses the need for the Lebanese groups to avoid the involvement in the conflict that may arise between axes in the Arab world, has unfortunately remained no more than ink on paper. All parties—in power and otherwise, as well as proponents and opponents of the confessional apportionment system—have snubbed this provision,

which shook national unity, spread chaos, and unleashed strife in 1958. This confrontation occurred between the camp of President Camille Chamoun, who supported the Arab countries affiliated with the US camp, and the opposition, which supported Gamal Abdel Nasser. It also happened in 1975 as a result of factional, sectarian, or regional alignments and involvement in regional conflicts involving multiple parties with multiple goals following the 1967 catastrophe. Similarly, we are presently threatened with such instability, which will become pervasive unless the parties evince a sincere desire for solidarity based on their realization of the dangers besetting Lebanon.

Religious and sectarian groups snubbing the binding precepts of the National Pact has undermined the foundations of our national unity, resulting in multiple conflicting loyalties. It has also questioned the sectarian groups' credibility and commitment to the pact of living together. This in turn has put the country on the edge of collapse and provided an opening for forces conspiring to dismember or fragment the unstable state. If not for the strength of the living bonds that unite Lebanese from different religious communities, Lebanon would not have survived.

Experience has shown that people who have abided by unifying pacts or covenants have been able to build flourishing, stable states. The clearest example of this is the covenant established by the ethnically, religiously, and linguistically diverse people of Switzerland. The Swiss Confederation covenant, which remains in force, came about after centuries of violent conflict among people with multiple loyalties. They were finally saved by the will of their leaders to be completely neutral toward neighboring countries and to stand together to confront, by force if necessary, any outside interference. Abidance by this contract has allowed Switzerland to remain impregnable and splendidly unified to this day.

A more recent experience is that of Singapore. This small state, with its multiple ethnicities, races, religions, and languages, united under its leader, Lee Kuan Yew[4], who was Chinese in origin and Singaporean in his affiliation. Within twenty-five years Lee Kuan Yew was able to bring Singapore out of extreme poverty into the ranks of the most cohesive, wealthy, and prosperous states while assiduously preserving the distinctive features and cultures of its diverse population.

A neutral, peaceful, pluralistic Lebanon is in the interest of the peoples of our war-torn region. They need a rational, safe space to communicate or meet with one another. They also need a social space that can alleviate their pain and deprivation. Lebanon's honest, objective, honorable part in such a role could be most useful in resolving the conflicts that are destroying our society and people, particularly:

- the tragedy in Syria, our Arab neighbor, where Lebanese groups have taken sides and been drawn by sectarian considerations into the cursed arena of conflict; and
- the existential struggle in the region between Iran and its supporters, and Saudi Arabia and its supporters. Lebanese groups have become involved in this struggle based on sectarian considerations, facilitating the spread of the obscurantist *jihadist* ideology into our country.

Close adherence to the National Pact is the only way that can protect us from being plunged into the tensions and conflicts that prevent us from playing our role and dwarf our message. It should be clarified that this neutrality does not apply to the Palestinian cause.

---

[4]   Lee Kuan Yew, informally known by his initials LKY, was the first prime minister of Singapore, governing for three decades.

5. Avoiding Confusion between the Ends and the Means

Our sectarian system has found moral justification in seeking justice among groups comprising society, lest one group feels wronged or deprived. The founders of the sectarian system no doubt had noble intentions. However, the formula for achieving the desired objective corrupted the state and excluded civil society. This led to the outbreak of strife and conflict, which has almost destroyed the nation's unity and the safety of its groups. Worst of all, the confessional apportionment system, entrenched in our discourse and national life, has become axiomatic for most Lebanese. The problem is that social axioms often turn into mental ones, even if they are wrong and defy logic. The mental difficulty in condemning the confessional system lies precisely in the difficulty of separating the philosophy of living together from the formula for translating this philosophy, which still centers on the division of the country, government, and resources among religious communities.

Given the confessional system's bankruptcy, is there another procedural formula that could replace confessionalism and allow for living together, equality, and justice for all Lebanese without reference to religion? This question is urgently posed because the existing sectarian ideology confuses the covenantal objective with the formula used to achieve that objective. Such confusion raises doubt about the integrity of the sectarian ideology, which fails to distinguish between the means and the end. Instead of admitting the failure of the confessional apportionment system as a procedural formula and seeking an alternative procedural formula, the beneficiaries of this system tend to try to keep this system afloat under the cover of the so-called consensual democracy. That has paralyzed national decision making and the implementation of the Taif Agreement.

Here we must pose the questions the political class has been trying to evade: Is the Taif Agreement still valid? If so, can the fundamental stipulation in this agreement be ignored, and why? Can the function of the National Dialogue Committee stipulated in the Constitution remain suspended?

If this committee has the opportunity to be formed, it will need to address the following problem: How can the confessional apportionment system in the government and public services be abandoned without violating our national axiom of balanced representation for Christian and Muslim Lebanese in the government and the public?

If we abandon the principle of the repartitioning of power as shares among religious communities, would it be possible to reach an alternative formula that provides the conditions for creating a national power in which the Lebanese groups participate equally, without one group dominating another? What mechanism can ensure the sustainability of this alternate formula to maintain the balance of power and civil peace, and function as a safety valve in national crises?

That is the task of the National Dialogue Committee!

6. Consensual Democracy Thwarts the Taif Agreement

Consensual democracy (the application of consensus decision making to the process of legislation in a democracy) is a heresy that became widespread after the freeze of the dialogue that was stipulated to complete the implementation of the Taif Agreement. Consensual democracy has been employed to justify maintaining the confessional apportionment system and avoiding the dialogue among the representatives of civil society. It bears no resemblance to any political system in the world. It implies disregarding any covenantal or constitutional authority that can legally and democratically decide cases of conflicting interests. Instead, it provides for a "consensus" mechanism to resolve issues between feuding sectarian entities. This mechanism is no more than a process of constant haggling whose outcomes are governed by domestic and foreign balances of power. How can eighteen or more religious communities agree on every decision or opinion? What are the criteria for determining what may be agreed by consensus and what may be agreed by a majority? Which religious communities will have a veto, and why? Can a parliamentary democracy stripped of authority to decide conflicts of opinions and interests have any meaning? If we were to replace the 1943 National Pact with consensual democracy in our approach to foreign conflicts, would there still be latitude to declare Lebanon's neutrality and thus avoid all the tragedies we are suffering today?

The assumption that a national decision can be adopted based on other than the principles of democratic practice, which require resort to constitutional authority for legal decisions, would likely lead to one of the following:

- the assignment of preponderant power to one community, which would then force the other religious communities to agree with it, as was the case until the civil war in 1975; and
- the inviting of a foreign authority to exercise de facto power on the pretext of maintaining harmony among the groups, as happened during the Syrian era.

There is widespread confusion resulting from the parties' exploitation of the political confessional system's misleading title of consensual democracy as a resonant slogan to thwart the Taif Agreement and as an alternative to the sectarian system that preceded it. To eliminate such confusion, it should be clarified that what this means in practice is foreign to what Michel Chiha had in mind when he adopted the expression *démocratie consensuelle* (consensual democracy). Chiha meant this expression to signify the desire shared by Christian and Muslim Lebanese to live together under their tolerant traditions and customs and the precepts that have become a basis for their common traits. The democracy promoted by Michel Chiha should more accurately be called *covenantal democracy*, which is based on the fixed principles and precepts that guarantee the equality of all citizens. It never occurred to Chiha, nor to any of the founders of the Lebanese system and the lawmakers of that era, to subject the daily decisions of constitutional institutions to a consensus agreement among religious communities' representatives. Doing so would violate the most basic principles of democracy, hamper political action, paralyze the government, and drain the economy.

A binding covenant is necessary to sustain a state. It is enshrined in the Lebanese social contract governing the nation. The Lebanese desired this contract to achieve their destinies. This consensus may never be circumvented or distorted under the pretext of the so-called consensual democracy, which implies the law of the jungle, under which national decision making is controlled by the momentary balance of power.

7. Recognition of the Pluralistic Nature of Lebanese Society

The experience of living with various groups that took refuge in this country in the past has allowed for the evolution of a distinctive Lebanese personality. But our society has again become fragmented into groups. It has been unable to demonstrate a unified national identity, not because we are incapable of loyalty to a future unifying identity for Lebanon but because of other factors (e.g., the geopolitical complexities of our position; the effects of our sectarian political system; and the effect of the malicious attempts to efface the diversity of our society and accuse of heresy anyone who dares to publicly declare his right to be different).

People who have endured colonialism, repression, and efforts to purge them from memory will naturally seek an identity that is based on a unified land, ethnicity, language, and/or history. However, the confessional system in Lebanon has not aimed at or desired the entrenchment of a unifying national identity. Each group has deliberately advocated for its own real or imagined identity to justify its pursuits. Instead of seeking to coalesce the citizenry around a modern state with an ambitious plan that weaves groups into a single national fabric and plays down differences, some parties in Lebanon and the region have gone so far as to theorize that the citizenry should be homogeneous and uniform. Such thinking is totalitarian. It is based on an imagined community whose members do not recognize or accept other communities or their differences. Such thinking naturally generates mutual fears and as a result, each religious community denies the right of other communities to be different and spreads fears of assimilation or marginalization.

Evading reality has led to the current tragic scene. Various factions are increasingly, openly, and unabashedly engaging in monopolistic projects. Sectarian rhetoric has increased. Religious communities are ferociously accusing each other of treason amid the revival of regressive *jihadi*, monopolistic and exclusionary ideologies that misinform about and reject "the other," their declarations to the contrary notwithstanding.

The denial of the pluralistic nature of our society has brought us to an impasse. The sectarian mobilization is a double-edged sword that affects everyone. No one is able to do away with anyone else. There is no serious chance of overcoming our existential crisis unless we unreservedly accept the pluralistic nature of our society. We must acknowledge the right of "the other" to be different and accept him or her as a partner. Accordingly, peaceful living together is possible only if we acknowledge the diversity of our society and respect its distinctive features. We will have no chance of creating a stable state unless we conclude a sustainable social contract that alleviates the contracting parties' caution and fear and precludes the resurgence of factional impulses to usurp and monopolize.

Chapter 3

PROBLEMATICS OF IMPLEMENTING THE TAIF AGREEMENT

The Lebanese are a diverse human mosaic. Lebanon is united in a national entity that has seen historical tension between two propositions, neither of which has succeeded. One holds that Lebanon is a nation separate from its surrounding countries; the other holds that Lebanon is either a temporary entity or part of a larger nation.

The tiles of the Lebanese mosaic could have been fashioned into a splendid tableau had they been integrated properly. But that did not happen. Lebanon never truly had a chance to properly compose the pieces of its mosaic, which remain rich in their diversity. The very fact that the mosaic had been preserved is a testament to all Lebanese, one that validates continued investment in Lebanon's grand experiment to fashion true living together, and a challenge to advocates of partitioning or isolating the country.

The strongest motive for the fifteen-year civil war, which has various names and explanations, was the injustice visited upon certain Lebanese groups, particularly the Shiite Muslims, due to the monopolization of power by what was then called political Maronism (the sway exercised by Maronite leaders and their allies from various other religious communities). The confessional apportionment system was actually unfair to everyone. This injustice catalyzed the formation of a broad front of political and popular forces from various religious communities, including Maronite Christians, who demanded equality and justice and rejected the preeminence of any one religious community.

The civil war erupted against the backdrop of the practices of the political class and the propensity of adventurers, opportunists, and conspirators, in the absence of a written covenant, or pact, regulating living together, thus spreading a demoralizing culture of division and isolation as a substitute for the nihilistic culture of uniformity and homogeneity advocated by neighboring countries. The civil war deprived our generation of many years and destroyed much of what previous generations had built. The horizon remained bleak until the Taif conference, in which circumstances and wills joined to end the absurd war.

1. The Taif Agreement: A Historical Reconciliation?

The Taif conferees reached a historical settlement to transcend the impasse. At the opening of the conference at Taif on September 30, 1989, the speaker of Parliament at the time, Hussein el-Husseini, summed up the philosophy behind the Taif Agreement in simple, clearly stated words that best embody the spirit of the agreement:

> It is a dead end for us to imagine that one group, however numerous or powerful it may be, can succeed in imposing its opinion and requirements on the other groups.

> It is a dead end for us to imagine that a solution that excludes any group, no matter how small in number or how powerless it appears, could be a real solution.

It is a dead end for us to lump together the contradictory demands of all groups and then imagine that this can reform society and establish a state.

It is a dead end for us to imagine that a state based on law and institutions that are at odds with the very composition of society can somehow leapfrog or bypass the need to develop society.

It is a dead end for us to impose a rigid formula that cannot adapt to a changing reality and is cut off from the future.

In this speech el-Husseini mentioned three Lebanese verities that the conference would reiterate and approve as a firm, solid foundation for the conclusion and implementation of the agreement:

1. It is unacceptable to give precedence in decision making to any group or to exclude or rule out any group.
2. Any formula that fails to take into account the composition of society is illegitimate.
3. Any formula must be adaptable to the changing reality.

These truths derive from the composition of the Lebanese society and its historical common precepts, including the Taif Agreement in particular. Those precepts require full, true equality among the nation's groups and citizens. These truths will defeat partisan or factionalist schemes, which are fed by fears of exclusion or domination. They affirm the preservation of a unified pluralistic state. They entrench its existence and distinctive role as the land of both Christianity and Islam and as a place where civilizations and religions can meet and dialogue without problems or fears.

The practical effects of the Taif Agreement were an end to the destructive civil war and the election of René Moawad as president, a visionary statesman who closely followed Fouad Chehab's approach. Moawad was a primary architect of the Taif Agreement and a supporter of the idea of making the Lebanese themselves responsible for implementing the agreement through a National Dialogue Committee incorporating intellectual, social, and political society leaders. The commission was to be chaired by the president, its tenets consistent with the long-held belief that Lebanese Christian leaders should play a decisive role in making any fundamental changes to the formula for governing Lebanon, as it is believed Christians are the most vulnerable to storms coming from the outside and are most able to deal impartially with the conflicting interests of outside parties.

Pending the completion of a plan for implementing the Taif Agreement, priority was given to calming the situation and mending the serious ruptures in the social fabric due to the war and division of the population. Lebanon needed to reunite its citizens and then work to launch a national dialogue to implement the agreement and entrench the state's unity, hierarchy, and neutrality. In this way, the state could gain the legitimacy it needed to modernize and lead society.

2. The Orphaned Agreement: The President Is Assassinated

These tasks could not be achieved without reviving political life so as to fall in line with the pursuit of the president and constitutional institutions to implement the Taif Agreement. The agreement was intended to serve as a solid foundation for building a modern, civil, unified, and just state that guarantees society's security and florescence as well as an individual's freedom and dignity. It was intended to create a peaceful democratic republic that supports the Arab renaissance and Arab unity and that distances itself from tensions, conflicts, and disloyalties.

The assassination of President Moawad was an attempt to kill off any hopes of the state being resurrected. It orphaned the Taif Agreement and aborted dialogue among the Lebanese and prevented them from realizing their covenant of commitment to living together and their desire to complete the process.

The Taif conferees agreed to implement the provisions of the agreement in two stages. The first stage called for ending the fighting and establishing peace, with the cooperation of regional and international players, without fundamentally addressing the existing sectarian formula. The second stage called for the launch of a national dialogue among the Lebanese without external interference. The dialogue was intended to reach a mutual understanding on a political system to replace the confessional apportionment system. The constitutional reforms were supposed to incorporate the precepts of the Taif Agreement for regulating cooperation and balance among the constitutional institutions and ensuring that they perform soundly. The Taif Agreement, a political necessity at the time, provides for a transitional period where the apportionment of power among religious communities is maintained. Once security and calm have been restored and the state becomes in control, the second stage would be immediately launched following the first parliamentary elections held after the signing of the agreement.

Unfortunately, contrary to what had been declared, the first transitional stage resulted in legitimizing an expansion and further elaboration of the apportionment of power among religious communities. It also entrenched parallel sectarian institutions with overlapping authorities, making it difficult to implement the constitutional amendments that had been passed to establish a procedural formula for a parliamentary system in a secular state. In fact, those amendments, despite the gaps they include, reflect the philosophy of cooperation and balance among the branches of government. They completely contradict the philosophy of the division of power among overlapping sectarian fiefdoms that clash with each other within a destructive, entrenched sectarian system.

The new Constitution was supposed to provide for a democratic parliamentary system that is based on the separation and balance of powers and cooperation among them. But it contradicts the confessional system, which is based on the apportionment of power among religious communities. This contradiction has opened the door to multiple contradictory interpretations among the rival parties competing for influence within the reconstituted system. As a result, power shares have been distributed to position holders acting on behalf of religious communities.[5] In this way constitutional institutions and public utility services have become sectarian statelets within the supposedly unified state.

Unfortunately, more than twenty-five years after the signing of the Taif Agreement, and twenty-three years after the constitutional deadline for commencing the national dialogue, we are still in the first stage. The constitutional law that was hastily amended to suit the requirements of the second stage has been open to multiple interpretations and as a result is a hindrance to constitutional institutions. The public domain continues to erode day after day as it falls under the control of the sectarian forces amid constantly shifting balances of power. It continues to be fertile ground for clashes and complications. None of the presidents who succeeded Moawad have desired to launch a national dialogue that would agree on a political system, complying with the Taif mandatory covenants, to replace the current condemnable system.

Lebanon's historical experience from independence through the present reveals an immutable truth that should be fully comprehended, namely that any apportionment of power among the religious communities for a transitional period opens the door wide to the permanent apportionment of power at the expense

---

[5]   The Christian president, the Shia speaker of the house, and the Sunni prime minister.

of the state's unity and strength. It also steadily fragments the country.

3. Abandoning the Taif Agreement Hurt Lebanese Citizens' Futures

In the post-Taif transitional period, the Lebanese public largely believed that the consent of the regional powers on ending the Lebanese war meant their consent on the restoration of the nation and the establishment of a government that could fulfill the Lebanese people's dream of prosperity, freedom, and culture. All Lebanese, including combatants, were ready to participate in a vital, pluralistic, civil state free of apportionment and sectarianism. President René Moawad was supremely confident that a secular state would be inaugurated during his term.

The principles of the Taif Agreement needed to be implemented with objectivity and integrity to enable the president to discharge his presidential role, unify the state, and launch the national dialogue in an atmosphere of restored cohesion. But this was not to be. Events conspired to adversely affect the political environment. Sectarian practices were authorized. Factional propositions were disseminated. The usurpation and crude transformation of the public domain into a sectarian arena were disregarded. Society was systematically corrupted, emptied of its ethical moorings, and divested of its role as a counter power.

Instead of launching a dialogue among the Lebanese to agree on an alternative to the confessional political system, some employed a religious extremist discourse, thus exploiting the elimination of political sectarianism as a sectarian weapon par excellence to intimidate a certain group. As a result, both groups consolidated their positions, further engraining sectarian positions in general and reviving dormant fears of hidden intentions to exclude the other group as a result of abandoning the confessional quota system, which had become embedded in the minds of Lebanese, by factional decision, stratagem, or coercion.

The abolishment of confessionalism requires a dialogue to arrive at a formula that moves beyond sectarianism and persuades all parties in the national equation of the need for actual implementation, not just theorizing. In order to achieve the aim of living together, the preservation of the rights of groups, and equal participation in government and the public domain by Christian and Muslim Lebanese within a civil, secular state freed of sectarian constraints must be achieved.

The Taif Agreement and the resulting Constitution were produced in a high-pressure environment. It was natural that the new Constitution would lack precise, unambiguous provisions on integrated, hierarchical authorities and responsibilities during the period pending approval of a system to replace the confessional system. Certain constitutional provisions should have been amended during the transitional period, but that never happened. The result was an ambiguous Constitution whose orientations have nothing to do with the Taif Agreement. The new Constitution produced an authority with multiple heads that was unable to act in a unified manner or make decisions. It became necessary at a certain stage for it to request the intervention of an outside power to regulate its performance and decide disputes among the parties comprising it. This was mandatory in order to avoid the paralysis of government institutions; the kindling of fanaticism; threats to civil peace and the unity of the country; and to emphasize the futility of procrastination in dealing with fateful obligations.

After President Moawad's assassination, relinquishing the implementation of the Taif Agreement brought the confessional political system to a theoretical dead end. The impossibility of establishing efficient governing institutions under consensual democracy became acknowledged. The only way out of the dilemma was to give precedence to one of the religious communities to exercise power at the expense of other religious communities, as had been done before the Taif Agreement. Such a course of action will not lead to the desired solution. Rather, it will pave the way for a new civil war that will find its justifications in the flagrant violation of the Taif Agreement's prohibition on giving precedence in decision making to any one community over the others.

The architects of the post–Taif Constitution were aware of these pitfalls. From the outset, it was clear that the constitutional amendments that assigned powers to the constitutional institutions, which are supposed to work together under a democratic parliamentary system of a secular state, did not harmonize with the dynamics of a system, which apportioned power shares among sectarian groups that have contradictory goals and purposes. The problem was not the Constitution or the Taif Agreement. Rather, it was the chasm between the Constitution of a democratic republic presided by a president of the republic on the one hand and, on the other hand, the archaic political system still practiced at the national level, which is based on the apportionment of shares among the so-called leaders of religious communities and the divvying up of the public domain.

Democratic regimes are based on the principle of full equality among individuals as citizens of the state, owing to the fact that the individual is the foundation of the democratic edifice. However, treating sectarian groups as the fundamental unit of a democracy is practically untenable.

4. A Crisis of the Mind

Lebanon is distinguished by its religious diversity, which is not usual for such a small country. However, it is not the only religiously diverse country in the world. Lebanon's problem is not its diversity but rather that the nation is confused with religion, and faith is confused with fanaticism. The Lebanese are united by their suffering and aspirations. Their failure to build the state is not to be attributed to backwardness or insufficient patriotism, but to the confessional system applied to govern the country.

We are not the first to complain about the apportionment of power-sharing quotas to the religious communities. Criticism of sectarianism has been part of our cultural legacy and history since the State of Greater Lebanon was declared in 1920. The leveling of such criticism is not limited to a particular party or political movement. Rather, it is widespread in cultural circles and among the political elites. This renders it a moral yardstick, thus giving it added meaning on top of its political meaning. Rarely does a political speech not pass moral judgment on sectarianism. The sparse few who defend the continuation of the sectarian system find themselves compelled to contrive justifications for defending their positions to avoid being accused of immorality. They argue that our society remains backward and unable to free itself from religious partisanship and must therefore adhere to this system for practical reasons until society evolves to the point where it can renounce its obsolete conceptions. They cite the sectarian and tribal conflicts occurring in neighboring countries and in the Arab Spring countries in general to substantiate their argument. They also maintain that other societies characterized by multiple religions, ethnicities, and languages have agreed on systems for power sharing among their various groups, such that our political system is not unique.

We are thus facing an extreme contradiction: The sectarian system is taking root and is steadily being entrenched by legislation, while the rhetoric across the political spectrum condemns this system morally and politically and highlights its shortcomings and backwardness. How can we understand this confounding contradiction? How can we explain this striking dichotomy in our public life, between word and deed, between the overt and covert, between what is said and what is not said?

Rhetoric criticizing sectarianism has certainly not always been honest and innocent. Leaders and beneficiaries of the system have in the past criticized the system to outwardly demonstrate their good intentions and exonerate themselves. For example, shortly after the civil war erupted in 1975, a dispute emerged between advocates of the abolition of political sectarianism and those who advocated absolute secularism. Neither group was serious about achieving its stated goal. They were only concerned with their power quotas in the government and their shares of government revenues.

The criticisms of the sectarian system leveled by the very beneficiaries of that system to absolve themselves of its shortcomings and failures do not prove that this system is weakening. It reflects the yawning chasm in our society between word and deed and between mental conceptualization and actual practice. The political system is not an absurd riddle. It is a reality that we experience, a reality that can be coherent or contradictory at times, one that has its legislation, rules, and policies with which citizens interact. It is a comprehensive whole that cannot be reduced to such dichotomies as souls versus provisions.

We are actually facing two crises. One is within society—namely, our unfeasible political system. The other is what French philosopher François Châtelet called *la crise dans la tête* (the crisis of the mind). It is a product of our flawed system, and resolving it is a prerequisite for dealing with the crisis of society.

Our current system has engendered a split personality among the Lebanese between words and action. This condition can be overcome only if another system is put forth, one that does not contradict the reality of our society, that is able to transcend the sectarian system without disestablishing religious communities, and that creates a separation between the political affairs of citizens and matters of faith corresponding to parishioners of various religious confessions.

Without question, the apportionment of power into quotas among religious communities has prevented the establishment of a modern state and even the possibility of establishing it. Experience and analysis show that the apportionment of power shares in the transitional period has failed completely because it unleashes a dynamic that gives permanence to apportionment between sectarian groups. It transforms it into a structural foundation for gaining profit and spoils and for political expression in the struggle for power. This apportionment paralyzes the political sphere in its entirety and regenerates and prolongs the life of the political class, further consolidating it.

Are we doomed to an impasse that forces upon us the indefinite continuation of the confessional apportionment system? Does the hopelessness of developing a brand of citizenship that is not based on sectarian or geographical affiliation justify maintaining our flawed system? Is history bearing down on us? Or does history always have answers and solutions for one who reads it with an open mind? Are we doomed to submit to this system, or is there an alternative?

The alternative system we advocate to replace confessionalism will preserve religion and prevent disputes. It will maintain the health of the nation, which is a requirement not only for the Lebanese but also for a world whose civilization and security are threatened and desperately needs the model of living together that Lebanon can provide. Such a system is within our reach if Lebanon has a leadership that can confront the rhetoric being used to feed sectarian fears, one that can move forward to implement our national agreements with integrity and courage. The crisis of the mind cannot be treated without rational discourse. True treatment begins with a political leadership that enjoys credibility and has the desire and courage to convince the Lebanese of the following axioms:

- Confessionalism, which has existed in Lebanon for one hundred and fifty years, has never been a guarantee for the life of religious communities.

- Consensus democracy is a heresy that has been promoted as an alternative to the Taif Agreement. It is no more than a struggle for power that makes possible the domination of those groups most successful at mobilizing internal fanaticisms or basing their influence on outside powers.

Clearly, solutions will not be easy. Each group will have to concede something it believes it is entitled to. The most important thing is that we all understand that no solution can stand if one group's rights are denied because of another. In order for a solution to stand, we must agree to trade our sectarian pursuits for an inclusive national enterprise; we must trade the mirage feeding our sectarian identity for a forward-looking enterprise that stimulates our national identity. Equality in attaining certain rights is legitimate; however, a better form of equality would be one that brings about a historical achievement that promotes our children's future.

Chapter 4

THE ROAD MAP TO IMPLEMENTING THE TAIF AGREEMENT: A SOCIAL CONTRACT FOR A COVENANTAL SYSTEM

Every great enterprise begins with a small dream. Can we permit ourselves to dream?

Lebanon possesses the fundamentals to be a cutting-edge, advanced state capable of creating a flourishing future for its people and for helping other Arab societies develop and advance. The Lebanese are in a position to propagate a culture of living together in a world that is undergoing demographic transformations and is vulnerable to deadly conflicts of identity.

Our country is geographically well situated. It offers an attractive natural setting, a refreshing climate, and abundant fresh water. Its people are hardworking and able to excel. They offer a large reservoir of intellectual capital and possess virtually unlimited potential to develop the country's information economy, tourism, and other services. Lebanese are diverse, open, and steeped in traditions of hospitality. They are able to connect with people and can effectively bridge civilizations and cultures to promote interfaith dialogue and harmony.

It is not an intellectual luxury to dream of a radiant culture and to work to build an advanced, developed state of freedom, authentic human values, prosperity, well-being, and justice. Our country's prerequisites for success considerably outshine those of small states that evolved historically into great civilizations. If we are resolved, we can build a truly advanced state. Within the space of ten or twenty years, ours can become a leader among the emerging countries, thereby realizing the Lebanese national ambition of being the land of freedom and culture.

1. Milestones

Before the Taif conference, the widely condemned sectarian system was the main reason for our lagging, worsening crises, including the inability to build a modern state. After Taif, the situation became more complicated with the unceremonious abandonment of the quintessence of the Taif Agreement, namely its requirement to abandon the confessional system. Unfortunately, instead of being abolished, it has become the one negative constant among the changes that have swept Lebanese society on all levels.

Our procrastination or dereliction of our obligations under the 1990 Taif Agreement led to an unresolvable crisis, where the state by its very nature has come to fundamentally contradict its Constitution. Through design or ignorance, a covenantal halo has been conferred on the so-called Constitution, thus precluding amendments for twenty-five years. There was a "consensus," by political and religious leaders, that the Constitution was not to be amended to fit the purpose and that there would be no return to the Taif Agreement, all of which has had the effect of again dragging Lebanon into a governance crisis.

The Taif Agreement affirmed a pact, which can no longer be ignored, by requiring equality and balance between Christian and Muslim Lebanese. It established the national goal of abandoning the confessional system by divvying up the public domain among the religious communities. It entrusted the president of the republic to conduct a national dialogue to conceptualize an alternative political system that ensures national equilibrium based on the following simple truisms:

- We cannot move beyond the confessional quota system without first addressing concerns, suspicions, and fear of unpredicted changes. Moreover, the system cannot be abandoned through coercion or the division of power on sectarian lines. The only safe way to do so is through an honest and courageous dialogue launched by the National Dialogue Committee. The dialogue must embrace participants, opinions, and visions from all segments of civil society. All must join in producing the desired historical settlement and the procedures for implementing it, as well as abiding by it courageously and fairly.
- There will be no chance of achieving equality among individuals and a durable national balance among the different groups without a permanent, agreed-upon mechanism allowing equilibrium of representation in the government between Muslim and Christian Lebanese.
- The milestones on the road map may seem vague and difficult to implement in the prevalent sectarian climate but not if we shed some of our preconceptions.

2. The Starting Point for the Road: Launching the National Dialogue

Article 95 of the post–Taif Constitution stipulates the following regarding the implementation of the Taif Agreement:

The Chamber of Deputies that is elected on the basis of equality between Muslim and Christian Lebanese shall take the appropriate measures to abolish the confessional quota system according to a transitional plan. A national committee shall be formed under the chairmanship of the president of the republic. It shall include, in addition to the president, Lebanese parliament speaker, the prime minister, and prominent political, intellectual, and social figures. The National Dialogue Committee shall be to study and propose ways to ensure the abolition of sectarianism for submission to the Chamber of Deputies and to the Council of Ministers. The National Dialogue Committee shall also monitor implementation of the transitional plan.

To avoid the confusion that surrounds the aforesaid constitutional article and to allay concerns about its implementation, the following clarifications, though they may be redundant, are in order:

i. The confessional political system mentioned in Article 95 of the post–Taif Constitution refers to the confessional apportionment system, which is the main cause of our distress.

ii. The abolition of the sectarian political system is intended to divest religious communities of ownership of the public domain and to renounce the divvying up of the public domain among communities' imposed leaders.

iii. Clearly, the basic function of the National Dialogue Committee is to propose measures that ensure the abolition of the sectarian political system. This requires a consensus on an alternative, nonsectarian political system.

iv. Article 95 of the constitution requires the formation of a National Dialogue Committee chaired by the president of the republic and comprising political, intellectual, and social figures, Lebanese parliament speaker, and the prime minister. The intent, therefore, is the formation of a committee comprising personalities independent of political alignments, in which the president of the republic is to have the decisive role in the selection of participants who are thoughtful visionaries, known for their integrity and morals.

v. The Taif Agreement set a deadline for the start of the committee's proceedings, which was supposed to have been twenty-five years ago. However, the agreement does not mention any specific deadline for the committee to complete its vision and measures for transitioning to the alternative system. This task was assigned to the president of the republic, who chairs the committee and sets its agenda.

vi. The provisions of the article 95, which is mentioned in the preface to the Constitution, are a covenantal stipulation that cannot be ignored. They require the replacement of the current political system with a system that meets the covenantal conditions for living together in a secular civil state as set in the Taif Agreement.

vii. The Taif Agreement assigns the president the historical responsibility of conducting a dialogue to approve an alternative political system and establishing mutual obligations for ensuring equality between groups and individuals in a non-confessional system. The president must also play a historical role in leading the transition from the current political system—which is the sole remaining legacy of the Ottoman Empire arrangements—to a modern state that is ratified by the Lebanese themselves. The president and his associates in the National Dialogue Committee must also monitor implementation and ensure that civil society embraces the new system.

The aforesaid clarifications are intended to underline the president's pivotal role and his constitutional and moral duties to achieve ambitions that might seem unfeasible. These ambitions are within reach if the president has the credibility, refinement, courage, and wisdom to implement what he swore to uphold without reverting to the logic of compromises and bargains. This can be achieved if the president is resolved to appoint our best and brightest elites to the National Dialogue Committee to shape a promising future rather than divvying up government posts and air time.

3. Covenantal Democracy

Democracy is an integrated philosophical theory based on lofty principles that have become part of the public order. These principles take precedence in the hierarchy of juridical norms over covenantal contracts, the constitution, and laws. A key principle is that citizens are entitled to equality and justice as an entrenched, natural, unequivocal right that cannot be derogated. Contemporary theories of democracy have expanded the concepts of democracy to include, in addition to individual rights, the natural rights of religious and ethnic groups and minorities. They also affirm that the alternation of power is a primary condition for democracy, and that democracy cannot exist if any one group is deprived of its right to equality or any citizen is deprived of the right to hold public office because of his or her religious or ethnic affiliation.

Thus, democratic systems seek to pass antidiscrimination laws and enact rules to curb the spread of divisive partisanship and factional tyranny. Democracy cannot exist in a pluralistic, diverse society that is vulnerable to divisions if that society lacks covenants that are binding on its constituent parts and that regulate those parts' partnership in the nation and the sharing of responsibilities.

The question is: Can we agree on a formula to replace the confessional system with an alternative political system that will achieve our national covenantal precepts and observe the lofty democratic principles of equality, justice, true representation, and power rotation? If we are compelled to acknowledge that it is difficult to abandon the confessional system that has become so deeply embedded within our consciousness, we should remember that this system was never a core national precept. In fact, successive constitutions in our modern history, including the post–Taif Constitution, have treated the confessional system as a temporary measure.

The logical response to the above question is to seek an alternative formula. It is widely recognized that a soundly elected Parliament plays the major role in power formation in democratic systems. The Parliament is entrusted with establishing state institutions, overseeing their performance, and holding them accountable. Can we imagine a procedural formula that ensures a balanced presence for all parties in a representative Parliament elected in a manner that is free of sectarian constraints? If this is possible, which of course it is, this Parliament could elect a head of state and speaker without regard for their religion. A government could then be formed according to democratic rules without regard for the prime minister's religion. The government could then be monitored and held accountable by a Parliament that is truly representative of all Lebanese constituencies. The president, his ministers, and government employees would not have sectarian immunity regardless of the religious community to which they belong.

However simple and debatable this discourse may seem, it is certain that abandonment of the political confessional system would require the establishment of competency-based criteria for appointments to posts in the administration and public sector. Officials would have to be impartial in their responsibilities to citizens without regard to their religious affiliation.

The answer to the aforementioned question lies in the method for electing a Parliament that is not bound by sectarian constraints and is balanced between Muslims and Christians. Success in this regard is the cornerstone for the success of the National Dialogue Committee. It is within our capabilities to have a wise, rational leadership that is above sectarian ideology and is committed to preserving the rights of citizens, regardless of faith, to freedom and dignity.

If a permanent, covenantal democratic mechanism is in place for creating a parliament that provides for national balance far away from the confessional system, then and only then can a unified, hierarchical, secular civil state come into existence. If it does, Lebanon will be liberated from the label of backwardness the outside world has attached to it. We will have a modern state similar to other people of the world rather than a collection of religious communities involved in internecine fighting. Individuals would be transformed from subjects of religious communities into citizens of a state with no need for the mediation of the sectarian leader. Government employees would be free to resume their role of serving citizens and the common good.

4. A Binding Social Contract: The End of the Bottleneck

The Lebanese have established the basis for living together founded on certain precepts. At times these precepts have been vague. At other times their covenantal nature has been subject to differences of opinion. These issues have generally stemmed from a failure to distinguish between a national pact (or covenant) and a constitution. Whereas the provisions of a pact or covenant cannot be derogated or amended, all of the Constitution's provisions, excluding those embodying covenantal precepts, may be amended.

We now need a binding social contract, a written covenant that establishes the way to peace and security and stability for society.

Such a contract will provide for the establishment of a state based on citizenship. This is the main mission of the National Dialogue Committee. This contract will not arise from a vacuum, as it must perforce embody written or implicit mores and precepts and treat problems that have long underlain fears and entanglements among religious communities.

The National Dialogue Committee must address primarily the following issues:

• A Political System that Guarantees Equality, Freedom, and Democracy

What political system can replace the confessional system while preserving national precepts concerning balanced Christian and Muslim representation without implying an apportionment or divvying up among religious communities? How can we protect this system from sectarian conflicts and the repercussions of fears and illusions that sprout up among the various groups and religious communities? How can we preserve the precepts of our covenants of living together equally within a state that is free of sectarian constraints?

• The Identities of the State and the Community

The Lebanese agreed on a single affiliation under the Taif Agreement after having experienced deadly struggles over identity. Clearly, there is no sense in trying to unify regressive identities. Rather, we must transition to a voluntary futuristic identity for the individual and the state. How can we agree on the essence of our sense of belonging—our Lebanese identity and our wider Arab identity? This would define our obligations toward both identities and preclude contradictions between our national Lebanese identity and our sense of belongingness to the Arab community in the Arab world.

• Nationality

In view of sectarian sensitivities, what is the covenantal formula for preserving our country's national identity and character? Is it legitimate to deny Lebanese nationality to individuals of Lebanese origin? What are the requirements for granting Lebanese nationality to others?

• The Separation between Religion and the State

The abandonment of the confessional political system sharply highlights the problems of the separation between religion and the state. How can we establish a secular state based on rights and abolish the sectarian system that essentially precludes the state? Can we create a state with values and a culture that recognizes the individual and the individual's right to full equality regardless of sectarian, ethnic, or family affiliation? How can we separate the domain of faith from the domain of politics? How can we distinguish between religion and fanaticism? How can we liberate positions in our public political and administrative system from the ownership of religious communities and return them to the citizens?

These issues have been disputed and argued. They remain the primary source of the doubts and worries that spoil our living together and open the door for conflicts among us or alignments with foreign axes and humiliating subjugation to them.

Obviously, there can be no economic revival, political reform, human development, or civil peace in Lebanon as long as the Lebanese do not agree to reaffirm their mores and precepts, including the Taif Agreement and the 1943 National Pact, within a permanent, fair, honest covenant that addresses the core issues that the groups comprising society still consider fundamental to achieving equality and dignity. The arrangements and mutual understandings needed to create the conditions for implementing this social contract must be covenantal and sustainable. They must not be subject to different interpretations, derogation, or divisibility. Any constitutional amendments must be made in light of the covenant terms.

Only then can we talk about the republic and its proper values or about a Lebanese political system based on a covenantal democracy.

Chapter 5

AWARENESS OF THE ROAD

When it is a matter of "to be or not to be"—of having a state or not existing, of having a future in the land of our forefathers or leaving the land—our only option is to boldly move forward, armed with hope. We have no right to level unfounded accusations at politicians or to suspect others and prosecute their *hidden*, unspoken intentions. Humans are pessimistic by nature, but history is forged by the will of optimists. If we try to build a better political system which leads to a better future, we may achieve our objective, but if we do not try, we will achieve nothing.

While writing The Road to the State, (Dar al-Masar: Beirut,) I had the opportunity to discuss with many citizens ways to emerge from the dark tunnel of confessionalism to the open road offered by the abandonment of our dysfunctional political system. Our discussions were spirited, objective, and unencumbered by special interests. The main takeaway was a fact I and many others had until then disregarded: The overwhelming majority of Lebanese, regardless of their affiliations, are much closer to each other in their concerns and aspirations than we imagine. I ascertained that what brings people together is stronger and deeper than what separates them. I discerned that partisanship, hatred, and grudges dissolve when citizens honestly and spontaneously discuss the future of their children and the honor of their country.

All the opinions I heard agreed that the dialogue can succeed only with civil society's involvement and pressure. However, there were pressing questions about whether such participation would be accepted by sectarian political leaders given their fears of a resurgence of public opinion that rejects the confessional system altogether. The discussion focused on the factors needed for a successful national dialogue. I came away with the sense that the most important factor is the restoration of the Lebanese equation of living together, with all parties regaining their role in this equation, particularly the Christians, who, in addition to their role in Lebanon, play a vital bridging role in the Arab and Islamic world. Interestingly, my Muslim Lebanese colleagues who participated in these exchanges evinced greater enthusiasm than the Christian Lebanese for the Christians recovering their role in efforts to fashion a joint future for the homeland.

My interlocutors were most concerned about whether the president will embrace his post–Taif Agreement role as the president of a state rather than the representative of a religious community. Would the president conflate his duty to navigate the country toward a safe harbor with his role as a sectarian leader, which perforce would make him an accomplice in the confessional apportionment of shares in the government and public institutions?

We observed that everything around us is changing, except for the very cause of our chronic crisis, namely the sectarian system. Our conclusions are not reassuring. The implementation of the Taif Agreement could be a fruitless journey into the unknown, unless we meet the essential conditions for the success of its implementation:

- the leadership of a president who is aware of the challenges and embraces his or her role fully; and

- the support of civil society as an alternative to the political class.

1. Awareness of the Role of Civil Society

Everyone complains about civil society being weak and marginalized. Some go so far as to blame it for the failure of our political life. This in turn gives rise to despair and a conviction that our institutions cannot be reformed due to sectarian and factional struggles in which sectarian loyalties trump loyalty to Lebanon. This conviction absolves the confessional system of responsibility for fragmenting our stricken society into warring sectarian groups and paralyzing civil society. In fact, it is this very confessional system that has allowed sectarian parties, bodies, and organizations to fill the national arena, leaving little room for the growth of civil society organizations and national parties.

The sectarian system is based on clientelism and loyalty to sectarian leaders. It leads inevitably to the disintegration of civil society and the revival of sectarian, family, and tribal ties. It makes individuals dependent on the family or religious group. Under such a system, in order to sustain itself, the ruling political class is compelled to entrench clientelism and to resist any modernization of social relationships, lest civil society become accustomed to democratic values based on citizenship, which would dispense with the need for a sectarian intermediary between the citizen and the state.

Despite the current situation, Lebanese society remains ready and willing to unify its ranks. They would appreciate an opportunity to rally around a rescue program led by the president and embodying the Lebanese determination to meet the conditions for establishing a state. The Lebanese are extremely adaptable, have outstanding communication skills, and are well known for embracing modernity and becoming free of clientelism and humiliating subjugation. If it can be revived, civil society, which is currently absent or marginalized, could become a salvation for our chronic crisis.

Today there is a growing popular movement that rejects sectarianism and the exploitation of the Lebanese in the conflicts of foreign countries. This rational movement of intellectuals, opinion makers, social activists, professionals, and ordinary people needs to adhere to a transparent and reliable national project dedicated to building the future of their country. This movement can be a bridge to a unified civil state that is keen on the culture and values of our society, which are currently eclipsed. This movement will not be a party or an organization but rather a state of mind characterized by a readiness to reshape and stimulate civil society when it becomes sufficiently convinced of the viability of what is being asked of it.

However, regardless of how talented and enthusiastic society may be, it is still difficult for it to play its basic role in modernization if its leading figures are not in favor of effective organizations. The activation of the National Dialogue Committee, which is supposed to include intellectual and social leaders, could restore the hope and spirit of civil society, catalyzing its involvement in national, intellectual, and political activity. The dialogue conducted by the president can moreover galvanize the entire political and intellectual arenas and stimulate and sustain the enthusiasm of economic leaders and social forces. Thus, dialogue among Lebanese remains the one means for restoring hope that the Lebanese state can yet be established. The civil society must play the primary role in supporting this march toward advancement and modernization.

2. Awareness of the President's Role

After experiencing the presidential terms of Elias Hrawi (1989–1998), Emile Lahoud (1998–2007), and Michel Suleiman (2008–2014), there is a prevalent opinion among Lebanese, particularly

Christians, that the presidency has lost most of its weight and authority and has become inadequate to exercising the required responsibilities of a president of the republic. The current president, Michel Aoun (elected on October 31, 2016) has yet to demonstrate his determination to exercise fully the post-Taif presidential prerogatives.

This view is supported by a comparison between the president's constitutional authorities before the Taif Agreement, which no president has been able to actually implement, and the president's authorities under the post–Taif Constitution, which no president has wanted to wrest control of or discharge.

The debate over the president's authorities has been heating up amid disregard for the substantive change in the Lebanese political system. Under that change the system was supposed to transition from being a sectarian hybrid presidential system, which grants the president nearly absolute albeit unimplementable powers, to being a parliamentary democracy of a civil state in which power is exercised dually among the constitutional institutions free of any sectarian constraint.

This debate grows more complicated when examined from the angle of the inability to implement either of the two systems. Before Taif, despite having absolute powers, the president was constrained by the sectarian balance of power. That balance limited his ability to discharge his constitutional powers whenever he tried to move beyond the mutual understandings and precepts of the national partnership. After Taif, no president has been able to act as the president of a parliamentary democracy with constitutional institutions based on the separation, balance, and cooperation among these institutions. Such a system, which is for a civil state that has yet to be established, assigns to the president, who is supposed to be committed to defending and protecting the values of the republic, its Constitution and its institutions. The president is supposed to discharge his authorities as the president of a parliamentary system. The constitutional institutions are supposed to cooperate in accordance with the stipulations of the Constitution; these stipulations are subject to amendment or correction. Clearly, such authorities are incompatible with the confessional system, wherein overlapping authorities fiercely disputed and the public domain is divvied among religious communities. When the president becomes one of a group of leaders, he loses his role as president of the republic, and the republic loses its legitimacy to discharge national authority.

The debate over the president's powers is certainly justified by the serious discrepancy between the current system, which has become more sectarian than ever, and the powers specified in the Constitution for a dual authority based on cooperation and complementarity within the parliamentary system of a civil state.

The Taif Agreement requires that Lebanon be a democratic parliamentary republic based on the separation, balance, and cooperation of powers. It stipulates that the president is the head of state and a symbol of national unity. It charges the president with ensuring respect for the Constitution and preserving Lebanon's independence, unity, and territorial integrity.

The constitutional amendments, which were approved by the parliament under the constitutional law dated September 21, 1992, particularly deal with the responsibilities and provisions, approved by the Lebanese legislature, for the constitutional institutions based on the separation, cooperation, and balance of powers, including the responsibilities of the president, which include but are not limited to the following:

> The president of the republic is the head of state, symbol of the nation's unity, and responsible for ensuring respect for the constitution, Lebanon's independence, unity of the Lebanese people, and the territorial integrity of Lebanon. He is also the chief judge, supreme commander of the armed forces, and responsible for negotiations

to conclude international treaties. He names as prime minister the candidate who obtains a parliamentary majority according to the rules observed in parliamentary systems. He issues a decree to form the government. He heads the Council of Ministers and approves laws or returns them for review to the constitutional authorities, etc.

The Taif conferees also granted the president an exceptional historical power, assigning him primary responsibility for implementing the covenant obligation specified in paragraph H of the preamble to the constitution, which is to abolish political confessionalism. Paragraph H establishes the abolition of confessionalism as a national objective. This responsibility is the key to the future of all Lebanese, the renaissance of Lebanon, and the radiance of its message. It is the path for preserving the nation, ensuring the security and safety of all its factions and groups, and providing for the living together. Depriving the republic of a president is certainly not more harmful than depriving it of a president who possesses the courage, wisdom, insight, and ability to reclaim the nation for all its citizens. Such deprivation affects all Lebanese, not just Christians.

After the Taif conference and the emergence of consensual democracy, the president could no longer be the primary decision maker. Decisions came to be based on mutual understandings, agreements, and the balance of power, instead of law and constitutional authority. Hence, the president's position will not be rehabilitated this time through the amendment of provisions but through his recognition of his own leading role, as provided in the Taif Agreement, through his determination to discharge his responsibilities to ensure respect for the Constitution, and through the sound performance and integrity of government institutions. For this the president must agree to preside over a unified state in which neither he nor anyone else has or demands a special share on behalf of a religious community, to the advantage of tribalism and favoritism.

Some believe—seemingly at odds with prevailing thinking—that if we should one day have another president like Fouad Chehab, who did not seek personal gain for himself or those close to him, such a president would not require powers that exceed those provided in the post–Taif Constitution, which grants the president greater powers than the power of a president contested and disputed by sectarian leaders as being the representative of a religious group.

The Constitution, by its very nature, is concerned with designing the political system and regulating its adaptation to the developments that are inevitable in the life of nations. The constitutional authorities must correct or abolish any constitutional provision that does not suit the state's current needs or contradicts public order or national precepts. We must put an end to the prevailing confusion between the Taif Agreement and the Lebanese Constitution, which many Lebanese call the "Taif Constitution." The Lebanese Constitution is in fact the 1926 Constitution, as amended on multiple occasions. The most recent amendment was made in 1990, after the Taif Agreement was concluded. It addresses procedural arrangements for the functioning of constitutional institutions.

The bottom line is that the government must be unified. The president of a unified state is the president of the state. He is not an accomplice to the divvying up of the public domain. Whereas it is necessary to amend constitutional provisions that are vague, confusing, or impede the president from discharging his authorities and role in balancing and orchestrating the constitutional institutions, it is impermissible to encourage the widespread view that promotes revoking the Taif Agreement based on the assumption that it has usurped the Christian president's powers and given them to the other religious communities.

3. Lebanese Christians' Awareness of Their Role

Middle Eastern Christians are conscious of their distinctive, humble identity. They continue to cling to their roots and to the land where their eternal message of love and brotherhood among all people arose. They remain aware of their vital, indispensable role in bringing together the cultures, religions, and people of the East and West to become familiar with each other and to harmonize and interact in order to live together in this global village in peace and mutual respect.

The Christian Lebanese are not a tribe or religious community within this Middle East. They have never claimed to be a national religion or racial entity. They have resisted attempts to exile them or separate them from their milieu. They have been driven by the belief that freedom is a goal in itself, without which life loses its spirituality and meaning. The Christians found a natural refuge and stronghold in Lebanon's rugged mountains. There they could exercise their freedoms and defend their existence and honor. They fled to the mountains and settled there as did other groups, with whom they lived harmoniously, sharing with them means of subsistence and human values. Christians spread across the valleys and mountaintops of Lebanon. They carved orchards and vineyards within the rocky mountains. They cleared the stones, leveled the land, and built terraces. The land yielded fruits and grains for them. Their difficult struggle to survive imbued them with a strong, unbending will, a persevering attachment to their land, and a commitment to defend it. All of these traits have helped them cope with the painful trials and tribulations they have faced with dignity and bravery.

The conspiracies, discord, and conflicts which the Christian Lebanese faced in the nineteenth century did not dissuade them from the role they had long ago mapped out for themselves, a role that transcends the geography of their small country and their own numbers. The Christian Lebanese courageously resisted the

Turkification of the Arab world, which involved attempts to crush and erase the Arab civilization and language from memory. They resolutely led a great renaissance to revive Arab civilization, for which they heroically and honorably paid a very high price. One-third of the population of Mount Lebanon was exterminated as a combined result of a ground siege imposed by Ottoman governor Djemal "Blood Shedder" Pasha, in addition to a blockade imposed from the sea by the belligerents along the entire coastline, and the invasion of swarms of locusts that completely destroyed their food supply. Despite its enormity, the catastrophe that befell the Lebanese Christians did not impair their resolve. Rather, it increased their faith in the mission they chose for themselves and their determination to be free of the problems that threatened their material existence and to realize their commitment to a spiritual humanitarian existence for the peoples of the region.

After World War I ended, the destiny of the people freed from subjugation was put on the negotiating table in Versaille. Included among these people were the Arabs, most societies of whom had been influenced by a renaissance liberation ideology, disseminated by Lebanese elites, based on a civilizational premise of living together in a pluralistic state that guarantees freedom and equality.

Patriarch Elias Hoayek was assigned to head the Lebanese delegation to the peace talks by the Mount Lebanon Mutasarrifate administrative council, with the support of popular leaders from the district and areas neighboring Mount Lebanon. Patriarch Hoayek was aided in his difficult mission by committees from Beirut, Cairo, and Paris. There were two options on the table at the time. One was to redraw Mount Lebanon district's borders to add Beirut and some regions in the north and the Bekaa Valley, which had previously been cut off from the Chehabi Emirate in the 1861 Beyoglu Protocol; thus, the new entity would have a sizeable majority of Christians and their partners the Druze, with the Sunnis and Shia remaining small minorities. The second option was to return to the borders of the Al-Ma'ni Emirate, which roughly corresponded to those of modern Lebanon and to annex areas that were majority Muslim into the new entity to provide more balance between Lebanese Christians and Muslims.

Each of the two proposals had its supporters. It was not an easy situation, given the all-too-fresh memories of the genocide, whose horrific wounds had not yet healed sufficiently for the population of Mount Lebanon to put aside its existential fears. Moreover, French prime minister Georges Clémenceau was opposed to the idea of a Greater Lebanon. This proposal would not have succeeded without the principled, unyielding stance taken by Patriarch Hoayek and the support of Lebanese elites living in the diaspora.

Much would later be written and said concerning whether Patriarch Hoayek had made the right choice. The idea of a country well balanced with regard to its constituent religious communities was unfairly attacked by other parties with a range of motives. However, the Maronite Church, like other Christian churches, was and remains today fully convinced that the choice of a pluralistic country open to the Arab world and Islamic civilization, a country whose role is counted upon in the renaissance of Arab societies, was the right choice. After the declaration of the State of Greater Lebanon, the Maronite Church had no role in establishing or promoting the confessional political system.

The Maronite patriarch certainly had no desire in pursuing the easy path of creating a Christian nation on Mount Lebanon. That would have meant cutting Lebanese Christians off from their milieu and isolating them from Arab and Islamic issues, similar to what the racist Zionist advocacy called for, which would be in complete contradiction to Maronite religious precepts and the Maronites' affiliation—with respect to their heritage, roots, language, and identity—to Arabism and to the tolerant Arab civilization which they helped shape. The Maronite Church, despite the rumors and ingratitude it faced, never abandoned its historical tenets that Christian values and the Christian civilization are the foundation of Middle Eastern civilization, and that harmonious, interactive Christian-Muslim coexistence endowed their presence with a spiritual and moral quality described by Pope John Paul II in his apostolic exhortation, "A New Hope for Lebanon" May 10, 1997:

> A single destiny links Christians and Muslims in Lebanon and the rest of the region's countries, and each unique culture still bears its own religious and non-religious nature from the various civilizations which came in sequence on its land. The Christians of Lebanon and the entire Arab world, who are proud of their heritage, actively contribute to cultural evolution. I would like to stress, with regard to the Christians of Lebanon, the importance of their preservation and strengthening their relationship of solidarity with the Arab world. I call on them to consider their inclusion in Arab culture, to which they have contributed greatly, a unique position so as to be able, together with the other Christians of the Arab Countries, to hold an honest and profound dialogue with Muslims. The Christians and Muslims of the Middle East, who live in the same region, have in their history gone through times of glory and times of despair, and I call on them to together build a future of coexistence and cooperation, with the goal of the humane and moral development of their peoples. Furthermore, dialogue and cooperation between the Christians and Muslims of Lebanon could help achieve the same step in other countries.

On September 1, 1920, the French Mandate announced the formation of the State of Greater Lebanon within its current borders. Under the terms of the mandate, France assumed responsibility for overseeing this emerging state and guiding it in building a modern republic fit for independence. The French Mandate facilitated the choice of a political system embodying the virtues of a democratic republic. France at the time was seen in the Arab world as an enlightened model of democracy, and it was natural for most people to assume that the mandatory power planned or intended to build a secular, nonsectarian, civil state based on the separation of religion and state, albeit without denying or excluding religions or intervening in their affairs. Actually, in Lebanon, a vanguard of elites from across the religious spectrum had been the first to dare to advocate reclaiming the state and civil affairs from the grip of the religious institutions and transferring them to citizens. They were also the first to expose the irrational delusions in sectarian ideology, which nullified politics and considered it an encroachment on the sanctity of religions. They also divested sectarianism of its sanctity and its status as a religious creed.

The call of Arab elites for a tolerant, liberated, open-minded, spiritual religious ideology was greeted with enthusiasm in enlightened religious circles in Lebanon and other Arab countries. Islamist thinkers such as Ali Abdul-Raziq and Abd al-Rahman al-Kawakibi courageously expressed this idea. Al-Kawakibi, in his book *The Nature of Despotism and Struggle against Enslavement, Cairo, 1902* wrote, "Let us come to a mutual understanding in Arabic and have mercy on one another. Let us administer our lives in this world and let the religions exercise judgment only in the afterlife."

Christian and Muslim Lebanese elites in Lebanon and the diaspora espoused a committed liberation ideology. They had integrity, courage, and the will to wage battle to modernize Lebanon and its broader milieu. They sought to free Arab societies from Salafist ideology and to rationalize their mobilization and conceptualization. Lebanon, they believed, needed to become a laboratory and model for the development and renaissance of Arab societies based on the values of modernity, particularly the separation of religion and state and the liberation of both from exclusionist ideologies and regressive delusions. These Lebanese elites played a deserving pioneer role in the Middle East wherein Lebanon's special attributes affirmed the values of Arabism and Islam. The Middle Eastern emerging elites have seen that this Lebanese particularity in no way undermines the Arab identity of Lebanon or its role in the renaissance of the Arab civilization, which has many sources and where Middle Eastern Christianity is a representation of the uniqueness, richness, and humaneness of this civilization.

The real challenge was to transform Lebanon from a natural fortress for the religious and ethnic groups that took refuge in it into a spiritual fortress that defends human freedom and dignity for all. Nearly a century later the venture to modernize and develop Arab societies remains troubled and enveloped by obstacles and dangers. It must be bravely acknowledged that the Lebanese, particularly the Christians, have participated in this effort and bear responsibility for what happened and what might happen. They also bear moral and ethical responsibility for the failure of the Lebanese laboratory, which the Arab elites had counted on to give insight into their path in their struggle for development. It had been hoped that this laboratory would become transformed into a model for emulation by Arab societies in their bitter struggle to achieve social liberation and modernity.

The belief that modernization would succeed in Lebanese society had some justification. Of the Arab societies, Lebanon was the most developed and in closest contact with the West. It was the most open to religious and cultural diversity. It had experienced demands for social change through struggle during the peasant uprisings in the nineteenth century. It also went through the painful experience of the fabricated sectarian conflict ignited by the conflicts of other nations in the mid-nineteenth century. These painful experiences strengthened secularism among the Lebanese cultural elites and gave rise to an ever-growing conviction that sectarianism was the greatest impediment to the progress and development of Lebanon and to the establishment of a modern republic. They also led to the belief that sectarianism is a deadly epidemic that poses a serious threat to Arab societies at risk of dissolution, if it can breathe life into the apprehensions and fears of the groups that make up Arab society, which is pluralistic.

It was expected that the constitution of the nascent Lebanese state would separate religion from the state, especially since the religious authorities, including the Maronite Church, did not object to such a separation. In fact, after a long struggle for survival, the Maronite Church managed to withdraw from the scene to the advantage of a leadership by the Lebanese republic in developing the state, modernizing it, and rendering it a most convenient space for the growth and harmonization of talents.

But the opposite happened. The mandatory power abandoned its secular values. It incorporated provisions with a sectarian bent into the 1926 constitution. True, these provisions were considered temporary under Article 95 of the constitution. Nonetheless, the dynamic of these "temporary measures" combined with the special benefits provided by the sectarian system to cause the failure of the Lebanese experiment. The country returned to its prestate status quo, divided into a number of homelands. The cultural and social renaissance was effectively extinguished.

The mandatory power, of course, had a role in issuing the dubious sectarian constitution. It would thus be easy to heap all the blame on France. However, ethical probity requires casting the lion's share of the blame on the Christian political leaders who led political power during that period and had decisive influence on the orientations of the mandatory power. Had they wanted, they could have convinced the mandatory power to abandon the sectarian constitution. Had they done so, history would have taken another course, not only in Lebanon but throughout the Arab world.

The breakdown of the Lebanese experiment and the resignation or dispiritedness of the Lebanese elites starting in the mid-twentieth century bear major responsibility for what happened in Lebanon and the Arab world. Concerning the Lebanese Christians, Abbas Beydoun wrote in the Lebanese newspaper *An-Nahar*, "*[The Lebanese Christians] grant Lebanon its system, and they are at the center of the state, the economy, politics, culture, and lifestyle. They identify with Lebanon, and they alone are able to make of their history and culture the prevailing history and culture.*"

To be fair, we should also point out that the sectarian leaders who have been in power are also responsible for the woes that have befallen Lebanon, and that the nation is in grave danger due to the persistence of this destructive system. Consequently, Christian elites have retreated from their pioneering role in the renaissance of Arab societies and the struggle for social liberation. Amid the resurgence of barbarianism, they are no longer setting an example of how living together can be revitalized among the different ethnic, sectarian, and religious groups, guided by the traditions and heritage of Arab culture in its golden ages.

For Lebanese Christians, the problem today is not so much the fighting over the scattered remnants of this state or the humiliating seeking of what is left of its wreckage. Rather, the real dilemma lies in the Lebanese determination and axioms, which have generated fears and illusions that are spreading malaise in their consciousness as the intellectual Abbot Boulos Naaman writes in his book *Whither the Lebanon of the Maronites?*

> The Christians in this country are in distress. But they are not endangered as is rumored, because the core problem in Lebanon and in

certain Arab countries is not differences in religious doctrine but rather differences in social affiliation and societal issues. The result is contentious partisanship based on loyalty to the religious group, which has repercussions on the political level. The way out on the political level is to develop a social sense of belonging instead of a religious sense of belonging, and to develop common interests, as happened in the past. This is what brings together the two sides and eliminates the social distances between them, mitigating the acuteness of the partisanship among them. We know that it is in the interest of the smaller group in the equation to take the initiative to develop an alternative, civic sense of belonging.

In order to extricate ourselves from the pressing historical dilemma, Naaman believes the only solution is to agree on a permanent, fixed national covenant. In the same book, he writes:

Now is the time for determination, and not temporary settlements. A settlement is an appropriate arrangement to stop a certain outbreak of violence. However, it does not form a foundation for resolving all of the problems of peoples. A firm rule would be an agreement on a national covenant based on unambiguous, unequivocal terms, with no malicious intentions; a covenant that would not be blown up from within or conspired against from without at the first opportunity.

In the preceding remarks, Naaman's thinking intersects with the historical solution provided under the Taif Agreement, which, under Article 95, assigns the president the difficult task of extricating the country from the fatal trap of sectarianism. The Lebanese people hope that President Aoun, has the vision, ability, conviction and courage to complete the implementation of the Taif Agreement and thereby liberate Lebanon from the dregs of its sectarian system. That system has fragmented, weakened, and corrupted both the society and state.

There can be no serious chance of extricating Lebanon from its booby-trapped sectarian system, unless the Lebanese Christians shed their humiliating dispiritedness and achieve their long-awaited historical promise to create a civil, secular state free of sectarianism and backwardness.

The current situation in Beirut's streets and in political forums and the sectarian struggles that have paralyzed what little remains of the state are symptomatic of the nation's malady and the severe crisis of the sectarian system. They also herald the possibility that the sectarian system can be abandoned. At the same time, a new situation is crystallizing wherein the main actors are citizens from civil society. The growing anger of various segments of Lebanese society will necessarily lead to the genesis of a popular movement focused on demands and free of sectarian affiliations, which may in turn lead to a political awareness that will no doubt entail considerable struggle until it brings the movement into maturation, thus reaching its goals.

A revitalized, nonsectarian civil movement focused on socioeconomic demands, given its potential to threaten current sectarian powers and interests, may pave the way for dampening sectarian conflicts. It would also incentivize Christian leaders to avoid sectarian, racist conflicts. Such conflicts continue to revive memories of discord from the distant past while blocking out more recent memories of daily interfaith ties that have united Lebanese Christians and Muslims. Ethical responsibility obliges Lebanese Christians at this stage, as always, to bury the hatchet, douse the flames of discord, and support both parties of the current conflict. They must be restored to the Lebanese national family, whose members must contend for economic, social, and cultural programs, not suicidal factional schemes.

For Lebanese Christians, the greatest fear stems from their belief that their numerical percentage is declining thus diminishing their political, social, economic, and cultural weight. The Christian percentage of the population has indeed declined appreciably since 1975 due to demographic trends, including migration, foreign naturalization, and resettlement. However, it is unacceptable to gauge the weight of the Lebanese in their country solely based on the logic of numbers or a census.

Abbot Paul Naaman[6] observed that "Christians wanted Lebanon to be a unified state when they were a minority. They also chose this option when they became a majority. They have adhered to this choice in all circumstances. Their loyalty to Lebanon was not affected by their number, but rather by their ability for a mutual living with others, including the Druze and all the Muslim communities. The standing and weight of Christians depends on Lebanon remaining a land of dialogue and of Muslims and Christians living together."

The Christian presence, Naaman believes, "was never about numbers, because the Christians are people endowed with much hope. They measure their weight by what they represent in human and spiritual terms to others. Lebanon has historically never been greater than it was during the times of its social movements which were deeply rooted in their dream of modernizing the Arab world."

In order for Lebanon to be resurrected, Christians must let go of some of what they consider to be axioms. They must also let go of prevalent ideas that feed their fears and apprehensions and are exploited to stunt their presence.

---

[6]   Abbot Paul Naaman is a scholar and former Superior General of the Order of Lebanese Maronite Monks.

The following truths, which are indisputably valid, need to be remembered:

- The first truth: Despite the decline in their demographic weight, Christians are still playing a leading role in productive economic sectors that are independent of religious communities such as industry, tourism, banking, health, education, and the various services. They are still heavily present in the liberal professions, media, culture, and publishing. Moreover, they remain the most geographically widespread community in Lebanon and in their real estate and agricultural holdings.

  Christian political leaders in the sectarian system are directly responsible for the decline in the political weight of the Christians and in the decline of the Christian elites' interest in working in the failed public sector. They have been unable to rally around a serious national program for promoting a political renaissance and combating corruption in the administration and public institutions, which would attract talented people to work in the public sector.

- The second truth: There is no point in debating and proposing remedies for preserving the Christian presence in Lebanon and the Middle East unless individuals can attain the basic factors for self-actualization and protection of their security, prosperity, and human dignity. Clearly, there is no point in trying to convince anyone, Christian or Muslim, to stay in an underdeveloped, wretched country if he or she has the chance for a decent life abroad. The opposite holds true as well. An economic, social, and cultural renaissance in Lebanon would encourage hundreds of thousands of Lebanese Christian and Muslim emigrants to return to the country and help achieve the highly acclaimed Lebanese miracle that previously glided away like a mirage. We were unable to hold onto it, because we have until recently been consumed with dividing up the remnants of the country, thereby depriving ourselves of the awakening of this long slumbering giant.

- The third truth: There exists no Lebanese group or religious community that wants Lebanon to be without its Christians. In fact, a considerable percentage of Muslims desire to see the Christians shine again in Lebanon for their own Arab or Islamic reasons. His Eminence Imam Mohammad Mahdi Shamseddine,[7] a Lebanese Shiite leader who died in 2001, said the following in his book *The Commandments*, which has become essential reading for the Lebanese elite:

Several formulae were devised, the most prominent and mature being what we call the 1977 formula, wherein we established the fundamental key principle in the political history of Lebanon, namely that Lebanon is a permanent homeland for all of its sons in order to preclude any Christian fears of assimilation. ... The fact is that this principle was established not only to mollify the Christians, but because it was—and I believe still is—necessary for Lebanese society and the survival of Lebanon as an entity, not only in the interest of Lebanon and its people, but also in the interest of the Arab world in many dimensions, and even in the interest of many parties in the Islamic world. This is added to the essential presence and dynamism of the Christians in Lebanon.

Elsewhere, Imam Shamseddine states:

A key recommendation that I emphasize for Lebanese Muslims and all Arabs is to be most keen on preserving the

---

[7] The late Imam Muhammad Mahdi Shamseddine, was the head of the Higher Shiite Council.

existence and dynamism of the Christians in Lebanon and on their complementarity and sense of complete belonging and full satisfaction, so that they do not experience any dispiritedness, deprivation, lack, diminishment, fear about the future, and so on. This vision is not based on courtesy and humane sentiment but rather on objective, basic facts that must be taken into account.

Has the time come for Lebanese Christians to revive their project for Lebanon, the country of freedom and culture?

Part II

A ROAD MAP FOR ECONOMIC AND SOCIAL DEVELOPMENT IN LEBANON

Introduction

Evasion of responsibility and reckless decision making at the national level have become an existential threat. We are morally obliged to together initiate a sincere discussion on our tragic economic situation, which threatens the survival of our homeland and our existence within it.

Our current situation is characterized by:

- chronic economic failure on multiple levels, which threatens to bankrupt the state and impoverish the population;
- growing emigration, which threatens the order, equilibrium, and happiness of society;
- the intensifying, unchecked degradation of the environment, landscape, and heritage sites;
- a corrupt, failed state with a flabby, incompetent public sector;
- a demoralized private sector that lacks courage, self-confidence, and trust in the future; and
- capacities that are paralyzed, disregarded, or otherwise idle amid a desultory lack of vision.

Despite the tragedies and nightmares of this reality, I must admit that I am optimistic, both by nature and by choice. Optimism is a chronic malady from which I shall never recover, not only because, like any one of us, I need a good deal of courage to carry on in this country and face the challenges of our distressed society but also because I see the other side of the coin and realize that optimism is a logical, rational choice, particularly as the changes we have seen in the world over the past three decades seem to be tailor-made for Lebanon's relative advantages.

We have unexpectedly experienced changes we have yet to fully understand. Our resource-poor country has become—without our noticing—rich in factors that favor our success in the global arena. Our country is better endowed with basic factors of development than such countries as Singapore and Dubai, which reached a position we aspired to in the recent past and could have reached.

In fewer than three decades, Lee Kuan Yew transformed his small country of Singapore from one of misery, backwardness, and ignorance into a leading modern economy. Similarly, vice president and prime minister Sheikh Mohammed bin Rashid Al Maktoum[8] transformed arid Dubai into a futuristic metropolis. Neither was a magician nor a conqueror, but both possessed courage, determination, clear vision, and a love for their people.

---

[8]   Sheikh Mohammed bin Rashid Al Maktoum, is the vice president and prime minister of the United Arab Emirates, and emir of Dubai.

Chapter 6

LEBANON'S COMPARATIVE ADVANTAGES IN THE GLOBAL ECONOMY

A discussion of the Lebanese economy requires analysis of the characteristics of its environment and position in the world.

Until recently, economics was based on theoretical axioms. Economies had a national character based on natural resources, accumulated capital factors of production, labor force, and the size of domestic markets and markets within zones of influence. They were affected by exogenous factors but generally retained a domestic character.

The state played a primary role in managing and regulating the economy. The public sector generally participated in production, monopolizing it in some instances, particularly in sectors that states perceive as strategically important to their national or economic security.

As a result of a far-reaching revolution in communications, we are witnessing a rupture within history; the future is no longer an extension of the past. We have entered a new age. We have acquired new sciences and technologies. We now use tools that were previously inconceivable.

We have accepted the logic of globalization, by which:

- The world has become an open arena where the rationale of wealth-producing companies clashes with that of the nation-state. The economy now supersedes politics. Multinational corporations—which include large, medium, and even small enterprises—have become the main holders and producers of wealth and key players in the global arena. The opening of markets and elimination of customs barriers have liberated corporations from the control of national authorities and has allowed them to invest and settle as they please in countries that best enhance their competitiveness in global markets.

- The growth of output, wages, and wealth in any country has become linked to the country's ability to offer convincing comparative advantages that attract foreign or domestic investors. Capital is thus no longer bound by nationality and other restrictions. It is available to countries that are proficient in attracting it.

- There has been a change in the rationale, status, and function of the state. The state's role has become more delicate, critical, and difficult than in the past. In the economic realm, the state's role is now generally limited to providing infrastructure and attracting investments amid global competition for investment, where only the strongest or fittest survive.

- Natural resources, financial or military strength, and vast markets are no longer the key factors in an economy. Wealth is now measured in human capital (i.e., knowledge and ability to innovate for production). Globalization offers new opportunities to countries such as Lebanon— which lack natural resources, large markets, and capital accumulations—if they are able to develop their human capital and adapt to the changing environment.

These major transformations are the very justification for my optimism, since what was previously impossible has become feasible. Globalization, at least in its economic dimension, has upended the balance of power and created new norms by freeing creative talents from regulatory, time, and space constraints.

Since the end of the Chehabi period in 1964, Lebanon has seen no serious debate among politicians, developers, employers, academicians, and experts concerning our country's comparative advantages. Such a discussion can pave the way for instituting a national policy to promote economic development and define the roles of the players involved in the economic development process, similar to what was done in the socioeconomic sphere by the 1961 mission of the International Institute for Research and Training, Education, and Development (IRFED, founded by Father Louis-Joseph Lebret).

The economic discussion in Lebanon has been thoroughly politicized. It centers mainly on fiscal management (public debt, monetary policy, budget, corruption, wasting of public funds, and other topics of debate among the political powers). It has rarely and then only superficially treated fundamental issues related to the repositioning of the Lebanese economy in the region and the world, which has seen astonishing changes in economic data, human development, government policies, and international relations in the past thirty years.

Obviously, global transformations, particularly in neighboring countries, have changed those countries' needs and disrupted the traditional role of Lebanese businesspeople. The recession and structural deficiency in our economy are the inevitable outcomes of the following:

- Most economic players do not understand the need to adapt to the new reality of the region and to devise a national economic development strategy that is compatible with Lebanon's characteristics and role in the region, which has changed fundamentally on all levels.
- Mistrust between the business community and political leaders across the spectrum has paralyzed or neutralized individual initiative and kept it from playing its indispensable role in economic development. The business community's frustration cannot be denied or disregarded. Moreover, our beaten society suffers from fragmentation, waste, and lack of prospects.

However, now more than ever, Lebanon possesses capabilities and comparative advantages that qualify it to reclaim the role that we have lamentably not worked to maintain. It is within our means to succeed, where we failed previously, to build an advanced productive society that can meet the emerging demands of the surrounding region and world, demands which are quantitatively and qualitatively beyond what we can imagine.

Lebanon's main advantages include the following:

- Lebanese excel in private enterprise, which is the main engine of the knowledge economy. By virtue of the country's location, circumstances, and open society, the Lebanese have acquired historical experience. They have thus become skilled assimilators, flexible, open-minded, adaptable, legendarily hardworking, and willing to take risks in seizing the initiative.
- The business community in Lebanon is distinguished by its ability to secure the financing for private enterprise in order to expand the production sectors or develop, upgrade, and operate public utilities.

- Lebanon has a surplus of specialists, technicians, and graduates who were compelled to emigrate. Abroad, they have been able to acquire experience and expertise. Moreover, Lebanon has no shortage of geniuses who are still seeking employers that can put them to work in the domain of services and production. Lebanese society on the whole is qualified to work effectively in the knowledge-based economy.
- The distinctive geography of Lebanon is still regarded as a comparative advantage by investors looking for a convenient place for living, entertainment, education, and health care, especially as the Lebanese are well known for being hospitable, courteous, and buoyant, with a propensity for an opulent lifestyle.
- Culturally, Lebanon stands out as a laboratory for living together and a bridge for communication among civilizations and cultures. It can thus serve as a unique regional hub for cultural and artistic activities, dialogue between civilizations and religions, and for humanities. Lebanon is also distinguished for its intellectual, translating, and publishing activities.

These are just a few of the many comparative advantages that can enable Lebanon to establish a firm base for exporting goods and services and creating jobs for our youth that are appropriate for developing the "other Lebanon" that we aspire to regain. We must take action to halt this disgraceful brain drain. We must export goods and services, not our precious young people. Most importantly, Lebanon possesses characteristics and advantages that enable it to become a producer society in many areas, particularly in the knowledge-based economy. This in turn will provide our youth with opportunities to stay and work in their country. We will then be able to export the goods and services they produce, not their brains.

Chapter 7

THE APPORTIONMENT POLITICAL SYSTEM AND THE IMPOSSIBLE ECONOMY

Clearly, the prevailing political system in Lebanon is essentially corrupt. A corrupt political system inevitably leads to a corrupt and ultimately failed state.

The confessional apportionment power forewent drafting a purposeful economic development policy for creating jobs for citizens, consolidating social stability, and meeting the basic needs of society. Instead, the paralyzed governments adopted a policy of procrastination, or a non-policy, in the hopes that economic prosperity would miraculously return on its own. And while waiting for the miracle, successive governments have continued borrowing to cover the spending of the slovenly, bloated government apparatus, which is beholden to the antagonist communities of the confessional system.

Those who count on an economic miracle assume we can turn back the clock when in fact the whole world has seen a basic transformation of its structure and fundamentals. Moreover, Lebanon itself has changed. This assumption is based on an erroneous mythical thinking in their geopolitical reading. It offers not a single piece of evidence that Lebanon is interested in or can regain its romanticized former role.

Such mythical economic thinking finds support in the clientelistic confessional system, which is primarily interested in maintaining high government employment and spending levels to satisfy cronies and gain supporters. The result is waste and extravagance, mismanagement, and corruption, the cost of which exceeds the revenues of the unrestrained government.

This system has led us into uncharted political and economic territory. Lebanese fondly recall the anecdote about a foreign economic expert commissioned to conduct a study in the 1950s on the Lebanese economy. He concluded that it could not be comprehended and advised that matters be left as they are without further study or analysis.

With the exception of the tenure of President Chehab (1958–64), the confessional system has adopted the ridiculous advice of the expert. That was fine when conditions favored the inflow of capital and investments needed for Lebanon's economic recovery. However, such a non-approach resulted in tragedy when the country became an arena for a struggle to survive, as happened after that hellish series of wars and tensions, which have led to homelessness and emigration.

The confessional political system, which is based on the divvying up of shares, has plunged the ship of state into a tempest with neither a compass nor a captain. The system cannot cope with the collapse of public finance, the decay of the remaining output capacities, and the bankruptcy of public sector enterprises. It has evaded defining an economic role for Lebanon that is based on a knowledge-based economy. Instead, it indulges, whether out of genuine conviction or just for public consumption, in the hope of reclaiming a romanticized past. The result is that Lebanon continues to flounder in a bottomless swamp.

Available economic indicators reflect the inability of the state to pay its debts, which could lead to bankruptcy. Following are some of these indicators:

- The national economy was booming between 2007 and 2010, with average annual growth of more than 9 percent and cumulative GDP growth of a record 55 percent, thanks to booming tourism and real estate sectors.
- Starting in 2011, the economy fell back into a recession. Average annual growth is between 1 and 2 percent. The economic statistics do not paint an encouraging picture: The annual trade balance deficit exceeded $17 billion during 2012–14, reflecting the deepening structural frailty of the production environment, which is affected by the deterioration of public utilities and services and the total absence of any credible reform or development plan.
- In 2014 the announced public debt totaled $67.5 billion. The public debt continues to grow uncontrollably. Debt service payments for the past five years totaled $20.3 billion, a sum that could have nearly covered the entire cost of renovating and upgrading the dilapidated public utilities.
- The annual operating deficit of the electricity sector has been $2 billion for each of the past four years. The World Bank experts estimate that electricity shortages alone have cut GDP by 2 percent annually over the last decade.
- During 2013, public treasury revenue totaled $9.42 billion, and expenditure limited only to public debt service, the electricity operating deficit, and government employee wages totaled $11 billion, reflecting the government's critical situation and complete incompetence.

These official figures confirm that the confessional political system cannot sustain its policy of irresponsibility and procrastination. They indicate that the confessional system is on its last legs, and that Lebanon has no chance of breaking out of its current vicious cycle without new leaders who can be trusted to draft a serious road map for economic and social development and who possess the necessary courage to take rescue measures needed and to stop doling out benefits to partisans and clients.

Chapter 8

THE ROAD MAP FOR ECONOMIC AND SOCIAL DEVELOPMENT

Development plays a key role in the politics of developed countries. A politician's competence in serving the public interest is measured by his or her actions regarding development.

Comprehensive development is a social need. As humans we naturally seek a better life for ourselves and our children in a stable society that provides a decent life and care for all without discrimination. Development plays a basic role in enhancing security. It curbs unemployment and homelessness and provides social safety nets for marginalized groups. It also reinforces the individual's sense of belonging to the state, because the state provides for the individual's welfare, freeing him or her from subjugation and dependency or from being drawn into extremism and terrorism.

Development plays a national role by providing decent jobs to the youth, which curbs emigration and encourages talented young people to enter public service. Development is an economic requirement. It generates wealth to finance the expenditures needed to sustain the development of economic infrastructure, meet the state's defense and non-defense needs, and cover the cost of social welfare.

The development process requires a road map in order to transition from a society characterized by suffering, misery, and loss to one that offers prosperity, stability, and dignity and ensures a livelihood, knowledge, and freedom for all, without all advantages or disadvantages redounding to any one particular group.

The passage to sustainable development requires a skipper, navigational devices, the will to set sail, and a clear vision. It would be futile to attempt such a passage or to dream of reaching a safe harbor without a ship captain who has a clear view of the course, is aware of our actual state of affairs, and is not affected in his or her outlook by what is said or not said or by slogans, accusations, and commentary.

Our situation is clear and can be summarized as follows:

- The Lebanese government suffers from a dire economic situation that endangers the state's security and stability.
- The state cannot secure the minimum financing needed to equip and modernize public utilities and cover burgeoning government expenditures. Simply put, the state cannot sustain itself.
- There is no real chance of reforming the public sector under the state's confessional political system, which is fundamentally corrupt and unreformable. Moreover, an economic resurgence is possible only if private enterprise assumes responsibility for financing the cost of the development plan.
- The private and public sectors are deeply wary and distrustful of each another. Such distrust can be addressed by clearly defining the roles of each sector and formulating legal, institutional, and regulatory frameworks for a

transparent, professional private-public relationship that is free of dependency, domination, transgression, and exploitation.

- There is no point in counting on public-private cooperation unless the public-private relationship is managed by impartial entities that are independent of corrupt political leaders.
- The deterioration of public utilities cannot be addressed without the private sector's collaboration to promote the sustainable development and operation of the public utilities within the institutional frameworks that need to be established.
- It is pointless and unfair to continue subsidizing the cost of services provided by public enterprises to the benefit of the well-to-do. The pricing of such services must be reviewed.

Based on these fundamental precepts, it is possible to draw a road map with the following goals:

- Intensive investments of the private sector in the production and services sectors in order to create more quality jobs to reduce youthful unemployment, stop the brain drain, and cure the trade balance deficit.
- Stimulation of growth can expand the economy, and the proceeds of economic activity can fund
    - government defense and non-defense expenditures;
    - expenditures on social welfare and social safety nets; and
    - expenditures on the development and maintenance of the infrastructure needed for housing and the relocation of citizens to keep pace with development requirements.

- Securing the necessary financing to develop, equip, and upgrade basic infrastructure and public utilities at an estimated cost of $25 billion over five years.
- Serious, bold treatment of the worsening public debt and high interest payments can be achieved by establishing an independent fund and managing it with transparency and a consummate professionalism to inspire confidence and prevent the state from defaulting and declaring bankruptcy.
- Establishing Lebanon as an economic and cultural enterprise that is indispensable to human civilization; and actioning on regaining Lebanon's roles in the economic and cultural realms.

Chapter 9

PARTNERS AND ROLES IN THE DEVELOPMENT PLAN

The success of the economic development plan depends primarily on the engagement of all forces of production in implementing the goals of the plan. The plan must include all citizens, social classes, regions, groups, and generations on an equal footing. All must receive a fair share of the proceeds of development and share in the responsibility of achieving development objectives.

The main partners in the development process are:

- The people: represented by the forces of production and the civil society and its institutions, they are the most important partner. They have an interest in shepherding and fostering the development process. They defend the executors of the development process and insist on the transparency of the process. They are committed to the fair distribution of development proceeds, and they protect development goals from professional demagogues, rabble-rousers, exploiters, and monopolists.

- State institutions (the public sector): They are the main players. The people assign the state the responsibility for managing public affairs, safeguarding security, dignity, freedom, and prosperity, settling conflicts among different groups, and pursuing justice in resolving conflicting interests.
- The private sector: Represented by companies, businesspeople, and entrepreneurs, it is relied upon to lead the economic growth process. It bears the expenses of the development process and produces wealth to finance government expenditure. This party is in a position to provide the investments and jobs needed to reduce unemployment and limit emigration.

Roles and Responsibilities

An economic development plan cannot succeed without a clear, explicit, binding agreement that defines distinct yet complementary roles for private and public sectors. We must also change the climate of wariness and distrust that prevails between the two sectors, which is the legacy of past autoschediasm and carelessness in the management of the public-private relationship.

Public sector institutions, the stepchildren of the confessional system, have with few exceptions become the property of sectarian leaders and subjected to the logic of the confessional divvying system, resulting in the squandering of public funds, which depletes available resources, paralyzes government capacities, and plunges them down a dangerous slope wherein there is no route for economic development.

The private sector in Lebanon is deeply rooted in our consciousness and mores. However, it suffers from weariness and weak initiative, which stem from the bad reputation it has earned under the effect of parasites, middlemen, and degenerates. However, it is neither fair nor useful to refer to corrupt middlemen and parasites as a reason to disqualify the private sector from shouldering its responsibility for financing and leaving the economic development plan.

Accordingly, trust can be rebuilt between the business community and the government only if the roles and responsibilities of the public and private sectors can be defined in a way that is precise, lasting, and agreed. Thus, the state would assume responsibility for the public administration and defense affairs, social welfare, and social safety nets. It would also be responsible for building and maintaining the infrastructure required for housing and for facilitating business using the surplus proceeds of development.

The private sector would be responsible for renovating and upgrading public utilities from the standpoints of financing, operation, and investment to meet the needs of the private entrepreneurs who will be relied upon to develop the production sectors. This is expected to generate surplus proceeds of development which would be used to finance state spending in the non-defense and defense realms and to create suitable jobs for the labor force.

Private enterprise has been the main engine for economic development. It has created what little prosperity our small country enjoys. It has strengthened Lebanon's steadfastness in coping with the challenges of wars, the frightening collapse of the state, and the state's continuing abdication of its security, social, economic, and cultural responsibilities. Private enterprise continues to be Lebanon's source of wealth and strength, its magical power, the focus of its people's hopes, and the country's sole path from confessionalism toward an economic resurgence.

A key priority for political leaders wishing to ensure the success of the development plan is to harmonize the two sides of the equation—public and private sectors—through laws, regulations, and institutional frameworks that regulate their relationship. This will enable the government to monitor investments, protect fair competition, and deal with flawed practices.

The state must also be responsible for providing an appropriate investment climate by:

- ensuring security and political stability;
- ensuring the existence of an honest and fair judiciary that is the basis for the rule of law; and
- dealing with demagogic ideologues who still consider businesspeople interlopers or competitors.

Chapter 10

PREREQUISITES OF ECONOMIC DEVELOPMENT

The global telecommunication revolution that swept the world during the last quarter of the past century has revolutionized our ways of living. It also created an alarming gap between rapidly accelerating substantive changes and the ability of the human mind to keep pace with and assimilate such changes. This gap can be viewed as the primary cause of shortcomings in social systems and of civilizational decline affecting the entire world.

These changes have resulted in the reconfiguration of economic and social hubs in the Middle East region, which is a vital ambit for our country. They have given rise to special laws governing the relationships between such hubs. Countries in the region, particularly the Gulf countries, saw amazing developments during the second half of the twentieth century. Their populations have more than quadrupled and their wealth has multiplied hundreds of times over. These countries have seen planning, construction, and procurement activity on an unimaginable scale. Large corporations have been established in their metropolises with skilled businesspeople who are in continuous direct contact with the entire outside world. They no longer need middlemen, translators, or business facilitators. Nevertheless, their needs for exchange with the outside world in various fields have increased a hundredfold. So if we decide to take action and regain our confidence in our capabilities and our role, we have to adapt our economy and our production of goods and services to meet the many emerging needs of our brethren in the Arab world and the world in general. We need to deal with these countries not as a labor market to which we export our youth but as an arena for trade and integration.

Our motto must be that our economy should be a need for our neighbors, not a burden.

We will not inventory and analyze the areas in which Lebanon enjoys a comparative advantage in the knowledge economy and in cultural and entertainment services. Transforming our economy into a producing economy will not face the problem of "economies of scale," for markets today have, in many areas, transcended borders and protectionist trade barriers, particularly in the knowledge economy, where we can play the role of a regional hub in a market that is well disposed to interacting positively with Lebanese entrepreneurship that is still respected.

The political leadership must realize that any prospective "Lebanese miracle," which has yet to materialize, is still possible provided we can meet the basic conditions for moving forward and avoiding pitfalls and traps with the guidance of a realistic road map.

The key conditions in this regard are the following:

1st Condition: Development Planning

Lebanon is comparable to midsized cities in terms of area and population. Thus, it may not need or be able to sustain its current large number of ministries, departments, authorities, institutions, and agencies in addition to such a number of employees, contractees, day workers, consultants, experts, etc. Yet like any social and economic entity and in order to develop its resources and promote a stable society, Lebanon needs a government that understands the complexities of the present and holds a clear vision of the future. With such understanding and vision, the government can prepare social and economic development plans, determine the feasibility and priorities of expenditures, devise an urban development strategy, and develop infrastructures suited to housing and businesses. The government must be able to prescribe the roles required of the private and public sectors. It must have an overarching view of effective means for ensuring public-private cooperation and integration to achieve development goals while avoiding overlapping and conflicting authorities, conflicting interests, or abdication or evasion of responsibility.

President Camille Chamoun founded the Ministry of Public Planning at the start of his tenure. This ministry remained restricted to the orbit of certain influential leaders and failed to achieve its objectives. It was nothing to be proud of. Nevertheless, it took the first steps toward balanced development.

After the war took its toll, the Council for Development and Reconstruction (CDR) was established and tasked with planning development. However, it gradually evolved into a project executive administration with multifaceted responsibilities. As a result, its planning role was marginalized, despite the important efforts it undertook. The abolishment of the Ministry of Planning opened the way for economic chaos and profligacy. It legitimized the divvying up of benefits among the sectarian and family leaders. It also legitimized the exploitation of public resources by sectarian leaders, who viewed these resources as shares above accountability. This led to the flourishing of "brokerage and middlemen mafias." It also opened the way for the approval of unfeasible, unnecessary projects in which powerful people had acquired shares.

It would be futile to expect the aforesaid beneficiaries to give up the personal gains which the system provides them, unless civil society creates an ideological climate that generates public pressure to establish an independent central development planning agency based on the following principles:

- Lebanon cannot avoid bankruptcy and collapse unless it uses its idle resources for social and economic development.
- Lebanon cannot have economic development and achieve what it needs without a constructive development plan that society embraces.
- The confessional system cannot be expected to formulate an objective development plan that is free of the conflicting and personal interests of the various groups.
- The only way to move beyond this grim situation is to establish a central development planning agency that is independent, honest, and dauntless. This may be possible in view of the current pressures, which threaten to bankrupt the country and bring on a collapse that will affect everyone, including the pillars of the confessional system.

2nd Condition: The Rule of Law—the Indispensable Insurance for Private Enterprise

Development requires abundant capital, which is plentiful in our borderless world. However, capital is skeptical until it becomes confident, hesitant until it becomes convinced, and on the fence until it decides. Nowadays, capital constantly seeks safe places in which to invest, meaning stable, secure places where the rule of law prevails and the state protects the rights of people.

The rule of law means that the state's rights and obligations are governed by unambiguous laws and fixed rules. Needless to say, the foundation for the rule of law is a judiciary that is fair and independent, guarantees rights, and assiduously applies the law.

Such a judiciary is a most important factor in investors' decisions on where to invest their money.

The judicial system in our country retains vestiges of fairness and honesty. Nevertheless, the overall system, in view of the abuse to which it has been subjected, is no longer what one would wish it to be. The business community no longer believes the judiciary, at least in its present state, can sufficiently guarantee protection of its investments and rights. Hence, the president, who is entrusted with upholding the constitution and the integrity of the state, must prioritize purging the judiciary and protecting it from parasites and politicians alike. He must implement serious, purposeful reforms covering structural aspects of the judicial system. He must reactivate long dormant inspection entities and affirm the judiciary's independence from the executive branch.

While the judiciary is the last resort in economic disputes, the government plays a primary role in averting such disputes. It does so by establishing legislation, frameworks, and rules that define rights and obligations, and by strictly and impartially abiding by them in its dealings with the business community.

Admittedly, the Lebanese government is unable to fund the country's public utilities. It can assign the private sector the responsibility of upgrading, developing, and managing the public utilities to meet the needs of economic development. Or it can exclude the private sector without providing an alternative. If the political leadership decides to commission the private sector to equip, develop, and operate the public utilities on behalf of the state, the government's relationship with the private sector must be regulated by law; moreover, it must aspire to and be convinced of the following:

- One of the political leadership's priorities in rescuing our country must be to support the legal, regulatory, and institutional framework governing the relationship between the state and investors in public utilities to protect the interests of citizens and the public at large. For this purpose, the government should seek the assistance of a competent, independent, impartial, knowledgeable agency that inspires the confidence of civil society and the private sector. The agency would be tasked with designing the legal framework protecting the rights of the state, investors, and citizens. This would prevent monopolization, market domination, and deviations that could alienate investors and block the privatization of public enterprises to thereby keep them under state supervision and control.

- The management of an impartial relationship between the public sector and private investors requires establishing a national regulatory agency capable of gaining the trust of the state, investors, and citizens. This agency would have sectoral bodies having the prerogatives, competence, and methodology to implement the strategy of the political leadership that assumes power.

- The objectives that have been set forth cannot be achieved unless the aforesaid agency is granted appropriate authorities and there exists a sincere will to enable it to discharge its role fully. This will avoid a repetition of the painful experiences of the present regulatory agency, which has always and still remains powerless and paralyzed.

3rd Condition: Development of Human Capital

The capacity of the human brain, with its accumulated knowledge, experience, and creativity, is the key factor for producing wealth.

Education has a special position within our collective memory, experiences, and mores. Knowledge is a basic means for the existence of our country. It underpins its socioeconomic development. Throughout the 1950s and '60s the declared concerns of student movements in Lebanese schools and universities revolved around demands for a better educational system to meet the needs of the economy and reduce unemployment. Those demands resonated with the political leaders during the Chehabi period. They facilitated the development of the Lebanese University and supported its administration's ambitions to elevate academic standards and prevent the unregulated expansion of commercial or factional educational institutions. At that time, Lebanon had been a benchmark for educational standards and comprehensiveness in addition to being a cultural leader in the region and beyond. Within schools and communities there existed a genuine awareness that educational development should be separate from the divisions of the confessional system, which are currently manifest in our schools and universities. This awareness arose as a counter to the political situation, with its multiple parties and constituencies.

At present, educational systems around the world have seen fundamental improvements, while our entire educational system has declined. We have witnessed a destructive, cancer-like expansion of for-profit academic institutions amid a total absence of the state and the historical values of our society. Had it not been for Lebanese parents' unprecedented spirit of sacrifice, and the students' hard work, our educational system would have been completely transformed into rituals and moneymaking ventures.

The logic of knowledge and education fundamentally contradicts the corrupt confessional system. This contradiction is apparent in the dichotomy between the education offered to our children in the prevalent commercial or regional institutions and the education that our country needs for development. Consequently, our economy is deprived of basic factors for its development, and our youth and graduates are deprived of the right to work and live in their own country.

If this shameful situation persists, and if we fail to find solutions for the ongoing emigration, that is emptying our society of its vital forces and youth, economic development will become meaningless and nothing to speak of. This treatise is not the place to present a road map for reforming our educational system. However, we should be aware of the following:

- Educating our children, which is exhausting for parents, requires developing useful educational curricula (i.e., programs that prepare graduates to enter the labor force and remain in Lebanon).
- Our educational system is no longer suited to the requirements of economic development and is generally unsuitable. In a knowledge economy, it is crucial to learn how to learn.
- In order to satisfy the requirements of economic development, educational reform must engage the central development planning agency, envisaged below, together with the economic authorities, professional unions, educational centers, research centers, and universities in developing educational programs.
- The political leadership must prioritize development of Lebanon's human capital, which is the most crucial resource for economic development and the generation of wealth. This means dedicating serious, special attention to public university and pre-university education, which are the indispensable engine for educational reform and the only option for poor and low-income families.

4th Condition: Integration of Economic and Urban Development

Lebanon's urban development during the past century was the most important factor in its progress, the prosperity of its people, and its social and economic development.

We once had a country with gorgeous scenery and an unspoiled nature, and a population—both rich and poor—that was hospitable, courteous, and had a refined taste. Lebanon was a cultural enterprise, a homeland of freedom and civilization. It was a magnet for writers, intellectuals, and scholars. It was a publishing house, a library, a theatre, and a communication forum. It served as a bridge for exchange on all levels.

We need to reclaim that Lebanon now more than ever, for the sake of our economic development and prosperity and to erase the shame and hurt that have befallen us. Globalization has resurrected the nomadic lifestyle for the business community. One may relocate whenever and wherever one wishes to find self-fulfillment. Urban equipment, cityscapes, natural beauty, and cultural amenities have become key comparative advantages that factor into choice of a workplace. The elites that produce wealth consider living and working in a beautiful and hospitable environment an inalienable right.

Today, the distinguishing feature between civilization and backwardness is the attention paid by the authorities to the elegance of urban cityscapes, the beauty of the scenery, the cleanliness of the environment, the resplendence of the heritage, and the vibrancy of cultural offerings. A knowledge and services economy can only develop if investors are convinced that the authorities are seeking to provide upscale living and work environments.

Accordingly, the political leadership involved in implementing the social and economic development plan must be concerned with the natural and urban environments. This requires

- halting the systematic destruction of the scenery, heritage, and environment;
- abiding by the master land zoning plan prepared by the CDR pending amendments thereto;
- developing programs and plans that improve the work and housing environment and forestall environmental hazards;

- adopting the necessary detailed measures at all levels to restore the beauty and harmony of the natural landscape pending reform of shameful, widespread degradation that has occurred throughout Lebanon. This is a difficult, costly mission, but it is crucial for our transition from backwardness to civilization;
- assigning a qualified professional body to approve the design of public facilities to ensure that they harmonize with their locations and are aesthetically pleasing; and
- considering Lebanon to ultimately be a cultural enterprise and an exemplar of the culture of coexistence or better said, living together; in addition to being a need for human culture at the wider level.

5th Condition: Integration of Economic and Social Development

Social development involves an economic objective, inasmuch as developing the individual's capabilities and providing for his or her welfare consolidate his or her sense of belonging to society and provide the shortest path to an economic boom. However, social development is not only a developmental need, but also a basic right in the International Bill of Human Rights. This right is enshrined in the preamble to the Lebanese Constitution, and the state is obliged to guarantee it for all citizens.

Religions attach sanctity to social welfare. Social welfare is an expression of compassion and cooperation among community members. From a sociological perspective it is a basic psychological need essential for an individual to feel that he or she belongs to society and fits in it. It is unacceptable to regard social welfare as a favor or grant that the state provides to certain citizens.

Developed societies anchor relationships between their members in a social contract that provides for a partnership in the nation and equal rights. This requires the fair redistribution of GDP among the partnering citizens. No one may be denied his or her share, and no one may monopolize the shares of others regardless of his or her role in realizing those shares. Thus, there is no room to debate the morality of, or entitlement to, social welfare or its necessity for the needy. The discussion therefore is limited to problems relating to the balancing of needs with benefits and to the criteria needed for this purpose.

Lebanon became a social welfare pioneer in the early 1960s when President Fouad Chehab tasked Rida Wahid with implementing the social policy that had been framed by Father Lebret, the head of the mission of the International Institute for Research and Training, Education, and Development. Wahid played an influential, active role in launching the National Social Security Fund in the face of across-the-board opposition from the business community and traditional loci of power. This was a pioneering experiment. However, it faltered when the confessional system recovered and moved to distort the essence of the social policy, which was based on the right of citizenship. Social welfare was transformed into assistance selectively provided by an incompetent, flaccid administration. Consequently, the promised welfare state was deformed into a clientelistic benefits state.

The new political leadership must prioritize reaffirmation of the basic rights of citizens, without favoritism or conditionality, as promised in that blessed period in our history which entrenched the rule of law and social justice advocated by President Chehab and his senior aides.

A question that is frequently posed concerns whether a resource-poor country encumbered by debts can cover the requirements of social development. The answer to this question can be summarized in the following two points:

1. Social security is not a choice but a citizen's basic right, which any proper state must provide.

2. The current selective spending on what we call social welfare, the systematic waste in public institutions, and the costs of the bloated government apparatus and public debt service exceed manyfold the cost of providing proper social security for all citizens.

The real challenge is not whether there are sufficient resources to apportion among the confessional groups. Rather, it is whether a national collective will can coalesce to establish relations between citizens based on rights and duties that are fixed and enshrined in the International Bill of Human Rights and the Lebanese Constitution. Among the most important of these rights are the following:

• The Universal Right to a Quality Education

Every citizen is entitled to acquire knowledge and an education based on equal opportunity. The government may impose compulsory pre-university education on citizens or their guardians to eradicate illiteracy and develop the individual's capacities and ability to be productive in society.

In this regard it is worth mentioning that two hundred years prior to the establishment of compulsory education in developing countries, the Lebanese Synod, meeting in Notre Dame de Louaize, Zouk Mosbeh, Lebanon, in 1736, decided to require

- the appointment of a teacher in locales lacking teachers;
- the registration of the names of the children eligible to receive an education;
- the ordering of parents to make sure that their children attend school, even under duress; and
- the church to provide orphaned and poor students with sustenance requirements.

This visionary historical initiative points to the basic values adopted by the priests to enlighten society as to the importance of knowledge and the distinctive role which education plays in Lebanon. It would be unfortunate not to be able to preserve this awesome legacy.

Specific plans for educational development exceed the scope of this book and are better left to specialists. Rather, we will be limited to emphasizing the role of political leadership and its citizen partners concerning the following rights and duties:

- the citizen's right to free quality education at all educational levels;
- the duty of the state to impose compulsory education on children under a certain age;
- the right of citizens to freedom of choosing private education;
- the duty of the state to establish rules regulating private education to maintain social stability and security;
- the state is responsible for enforcing compliance with educational standards in private institutions. The state may not cede this role to for-profit educational institutions; and
- the state must focus educational curricula on preparing students for the knowledge economy and on fostering a culture of living together.

• Universal Health Coverage

In addition to the fact that its economic return exceeds its cost, health care—protection, prevention, and medical treatment—is a natural right for people, because life is precious and socially and religiously sanctified.

There is a national consensus that our lagging health care benefits are an undeserved national disgrace. In fact, the health sector expenditures in Lebanon total 12 percent of GDP, which is higher than in any other country.

Health care is provided on a selective ad hoc basis by a collection of institutions headed by the Ministry of Public Health, which perceives health care as a favor rather than a right. These institutions include the Ministry of Social Affairs, which sees health care as a voluntary act of charity; the National Social Security Fund, whose will and vision have been paralyzed; the Civil Servants Cooperative; the army and security forces cooperatives; and a host of other funds and cooperatives.

The total expenditure of these institutions surpasses the cost that would be entailed by covering all citizens under a health care card system or universal health care system, if such a system is supervised by a competent board that monitors and controls spending in hospitals, treatment institutions, administrations, and the pharmaceutical sector.

Lebanon has a good reputation regionally and globally for its skilled medical staff, private and university hospitals, number of hospital beds equipped with the latest technology, and competent, courteous medical staff. Lebanon is qualified to become a regional medical care and medical education center if we can move beyond the disgraceful situation of greed and unhealthy profiteering.

The problem of providing universal health care does not stem from the unavailability of financial and technical resources but rather from a lack of will and from private interests that diverge from the public interest.

The political leadership that will assume responsibility for our future will have to consider the following:

- The overall medical fee paid by the Lebanese society is among the highest in the world, whereas the social output of health care in Lebanon is deplorably deficient.
- The Lebanese government must provide free universal health care as a right of citizens. It should establish a

detailed national database on the economic situation of individuals and families with a view toward distributing the free health care card to persons who need it, without selectivity or the need for mediation.

- It is believed that the cost of providing free health care for needy groups unable to afford health insurance is less than what the government is paying now in wasteful and corrupt expenditures and favors.

- In order for health institutions to function in an orderly manner, it is necessary to assign a national board to supervise spending by all health institutions contracted by the state. This board would be assisted by a monitoring agency recognized for its integrity and competence.

- The Lebanese health sector is one of the pillars of the knowledge economy, because it can attract highly profitable medical tourism.

• The Right to a Decent Life—Social Safety Nets

Low-income groups in Lebanon face subsistence difficulties and unstable and harsh conditions that are constantly worsening even as our communities generate greater wealth, luxury, and prosperity.

A significant number of unemployed, elderly, homeless, and special needs people lack a regular income source or face a fixed wage or limited welfare. This number is estimated at one-fourth of the national population. While acute hunger or critical deprivation are virtually absent in Lebanon, everyone has a sense of diminished human dignity, which has exacerbated feelings of humiliation and exclusion.

Our isolated rural communities, which are a repository of moral and traditional values, would not have been able to survive and maintain their stability had it not been for their sense of mutual responsibility and solidarity, which is embodied in their social, political, family, and tribal system. Unfortunately, the clientelistic system has distorted the moral essence of giving, transforming it into bribery or charity to attract supporters and followers.

These changes in our society have created a network of pathologically corrupt social relationships between "benefactors" and beneficiaries of "favors." Both parties are harmed in such relationships. The beneficiary feels the charity comes at the humiliating moral price of an affront to his or her dignity, and he or she harbors a sense of iniquity and resentment. The benefactor is tempted to feel a sense of greatness and superiority. He or she believes that what he or she has given entitles him or her to take something in return, even public funds.

A secure way to establish social solidarity and mutual responsibility is to redistribute GDP by taxing corporate profits. This will enable the state to uphold its social welfare obligations to needy groups without making such groups feel dependent or humiliated.

A common view among Lebanese circles claims that had President Chehab succeeded in implementing his reform plan and further developing it to eliminate the clientelistic system, the state alone would have been responsible for the welfare and dignity of its people. In that case, there would have been no need for benefactors and disadvantaged beneficiaries, which would have precluded the conditions that led to the devastating civil war.

Activists assume that as long as individuals are currently providing the basic needs of marginalized groups, the state may collect the corporate profit tax owed and distribute it through the social safety net.

It is time to stop promoting unproductive ideas and fabricating excuses to evade our moral social welfare duty, which is a leading issue that will govern the future stability of our country and the security of our society. The state must bear full responsibility to provide for the welfare of its citizens and preserve their basic rights, the most important of which are:

- The right to a pension that preserves the dignity of the elderly. The pension system in Lebanon covers only civil servants and practitioners of certain liberal professions. It covers approximately one-quarter of retirees. Consequently, a large percentage of the elderly are denied a secure source of income that protects them from destitution. The National Social Security Fund (NSSF) did not convert the severance pay system into a pension system for eligible persons. Such a conversion is certainly feasible, as there are only two retired people for every twenty-five active employees registered with the NSSF. This means that the NSSF can, if it so wishes, approve a retirement plan for employees who are registered with it instead of severance pay.

- The right of marginalized groups to a minimum income. It is absolutely unacceptable for segments of our society to lack a social protection system that provides them with subsistence. The cost of the social security required for providing a monthly allowance to the elderly, unemployed, marginalized, disabled, and homeless is much lower than the cost of subsidizing certain services that the needy rarely use. The estimated number of individuals and families urgently requiring social protection does not exceed two hundred thousand cases. The social safety net requires $0.5 billion yearly to provide monthly allowances valued at $225 to $375 Lebanese pounds. This amount is less than 25 percent of the annual deficit in the national electricity bill, which includes a subsidy that largely benefits well-to-do persons and mafias, who exploit the management crisis in the electricity sector.

- The right to housing. The state can do much in the realm of social welfare, especially in supporting the right to acquire a dwelling. It would be advantageous and fair to finance housing programs with revenues from a new tax on real estate betterment, which would dampen real estate speculation and the unwarranted rise in home prices.

6th Condition: Integration of the Development Plan and Infrastructure Adequacy

The state is duty bound to provide public utilities that meet the needs of the revenue-producing business community. However, the state is not a successful entrepreneur and cannot keep pace with the private sector in equipping, managing, and operating public facilities in terms of quality, cost, or efficiency. Therefore, developed countries consistently entrust the private sector with these responsibilities through privatization, partnerships, management and operation contracts, or build-operate-transfer contracts. This necessitates the enactment of a system of legislation and institutional frameworks that enable the relevant public administrations to monitor the proper implementation of mutual contractual obligations between the public and private sectors. Such a system enables the state to protect the public interest. It also inspires the hesitant private sector with the confidence it needs to invest in public utilities.

Lebanon's infrastructure is currently inadequate for development needs. It has been declining rapidly since the end of the post–civil war reconstruction boom, when infrastructure upgrading and development halted. The infrastructure has been maintained only on an ad hoc basis in view of the limited availability of technical, administrative, and financial resources.

The declining efficiency and lack of public utilities necessary for economic growth are a barrier that precludes the attraction of the investments needed to stimulate development and create appropriate jobs to ease unemployment. For example, the national electricity crisis is straining the state treasury. The cumulative deficit of the state-owned Electricite du Liban accounts for 42 percent of the total public debt. Poor power supply reduces GDP growth by more than 2 percent annually. Electricity generation pollutes Lebanon's environment. Lebanon's energy sector has been ranked the least efficient among 148 countries, as has its telecommunication sector. This tragic situation applies to most other sectors, including Beirut Airport, which is outdated and neglected and now subject to tight monitoring by international aviation organizations, such that it is feared that it will be removed from the list of accredited airports.

Clearly, Lebanon has no hope of achieving an economic revival if the business sector lacks the minimum public utilities needed to launch manufacturing and housing projects and to conduct business in general. Prospective investors in the information economy will certainly want to evaluate the adequacy of the information technology system in Lebanon before channeling their investments into the country. The same holds for investment in industry, where the electricity crisis is impeding the establishment of new projects, which largely explains Lebanon's significant trade balance deficit, which exceeds $18 billion yearly (37 percent of GDP).

There is no point in vacillating, lest we become paralyzed. Nor should we flee forward, lest we become disoriented. Lebanon needs to invest at least $25 billion over the next five years on upgrading, developing, and expanding public utilities. Without decisive action to pass a realistic five-year reconstruction plan, we may lose our last opportunity to regain Lebanon's position and role.

Passing an ambitious, courageous social and economic development plan will restore the confidence of countries, organizations, and economic institutions in our resolve to rebound and in Lebanon's future. It will also encourage organizations and donor countries to offer more support and aid.

More importantly, the development plan will restore the people's trust in their political leadership when they see that it is concerned about their daily living issues and prosperity. This will allow young people to feel confident about the future. It could spawn an ideological movement that prepares the ground for popular and youthful support for the restoration of the nation as a cultural and economic enterprise for all of its people and the peoples of the region.

The political leadership that will eventually assume responsibility for social and economic development must have the courage to inform the Lebanese about our grim situation. The leadership can rely on civil society and the people to embrace the complex and overlapping process of political and administrative reform, which must be dealt with sooner or later.

The harsh reality needs to be revealed in a frank bold declaration, as a first step in a long journey. This declaration should include the following points:

- Public utilities are deteriorating and risk going completely out of service in the near future. Economic development, which requires considerable investment and financing, is impossible without an infrastructure that facilitates business activity.
- The Lebanese government lacks the resources and competence to finance and operate public utilities.
- The political leadership is urged to assign the private sector responsibility for financing, executing, and operating public facilities, which the government is unable to carry out nor has an interest in doing so.
- Based on a prevailing discourse within our society, the Lebanese have justified concerns about the private sector

owning, being a partner in, operating as a proxy, or investing in a public utility.

- Legal, regulatory, and operational frameworks must be created for managing the public-private relationship in a transparent, impartial manner that is reassuring to citizens and is perceived by investors as a guarantee that they will recoup their investments and preserve their rights.

- The development plan cannot succeed unless its implementation is entrusted to qualified business leaders and entities, with the consent of the political parties. Such leaders and entities must be free of the domination of confessional powerbrokers. The existential challenge facing our future on this land requires us, at this critical stage at least, to be keen on the sound selection of entities and agencies that will guarantee success, particularly:

  - The central development planning agency, the first station on the road to development. It is crucial for a sound transition.

  - A national regulatory board will manage the implementation of contracts between the private sector, the state, and state-owned companies. The envisaged public-private partnership or cooperation can succeed only with such a board, which is mandatory for the private sector.

  - Supervisory entities, particularly the Court of Audit, Corps of Inspection, Public Tendering Administration, the Civil Service Administration, and other councils and authorities must be reorganized, restructured, protected, and empowered to handle their roles.

  - Courts and judicial authorities are responsible for the protection of the rights of investors and citizens. The priority of providing an objective and neutral framework to apply the rule of law is a prerequisite for a sustainable economic development.

The most important line of action is to galvanize civil society organizations to play their role as a counterpower to the prevailing confessional system in order to monitor implementation of the development plan, hold wrongdoers and their colluders accountable, and correct erroneous courses of action by engaging public opinion.

In summary, we must acknowledge that high steady growth rates are needed to generate a surplus for financing public expenditures; meanwhile, the private sector must assume the lion's share of the responsibility for providing the public utilities needed for economic growth.

However, the private sector will not assume its desired role and responsibilities unless it is convinced that the new political leadership is keen on encouraging private enterprise. To this end, the political leadership must courageously and confidently declare that the private sector is a primary development partner and provide an appropriate role for it. Moreover, it must entrust the management of the development plan to entities and organizations that are free of the domination of confessional parties. It must provide for transparency and integrity in the management of the public-private relationship to reassure the public, whose support and embrace of the development plan are essential.

We do not believe that it would be difficult to cover the cost of the urgent public utilities based on the availability of funds within Lebanon, on the capabilities of the Lebanese business community, and on the experiences of countries that have problems similar to our own. In proceeding with the development plan, it will be possible to secure the financing required for equipment and upgrades, estimated at $25 billion, from the following sources:

- fifteen billion dollars in investments from the private sector for rehabilitating and upgrading service facilities based on build-operate-transfer contracts and public-private partnership contracts;
- five billion dollars provided by international organizations and friendly countries in the form of assistance, gifts, and soft loans to finance environment protection projects, amelioration of disfigured landscape, and economic, social, and cultural development projects; and
- five billion dollars in treasury revenues from the surplus generated by the public utility development plan. These funds will be used to finance infrastructure projects that need not be implemented by the private sector, and projects that are implemented through public-private partnerships.

Chapter 11

REFORM OF PUBLIC ENTERPRISES AND COMPANIES

Public enterprises have collapsed and gone bankrupt. These enterprises are divided up among influential sectarian figures that have milked them dry for their own personal interests and the interests of their clients.

Public enterprises have become beholden and politicized. The standard of their services has declined as they have disintegrated, straining the budgets of the government and households as costs rise due to waste, corruption, and neglect. Privatization, which has become the magical recipe for recovery in people's minds, entails selling utilities run by the public sector to the private sector. This trend, which is global, is justified by the private sector's greater ability to manage economic affairs.

Privatization, while offering recognized economic benefits, may also entail serious political risks, especially in a small country such as Lebanon. The transfer of ownership of public institutions (electricity, water, communications, transportation, airports, ports, etc.) to private entities grants these entities considerable leverage in any confrontation or conflict of interest with the government. When a small, fragile country relinquishes its standing in any field, it cedes some of its power to financial interests that may exercise undue influence on its decisions at the expense of the public interest.

The national interest requires us to devise quick solutions to avoid total bankruptcy of the state, along with solutions for operating our utilities efficiently in cooperation with the private sector. However, we need not transfer public assets to the private sector unless the state has no interest in those assets.

Accordingly, privatization should be undertaken only under strict controls that preclude rendering public enterprise into private property. Moreover, it is useless to privatize public utilities whose value has declined to low levels due to mismanagement and accumulated losses. The management of such utilities should be assigned to companies that can competently operate them and restore them to profitability.

If it is decided to privatize a public enterprise, it would be advisable to convert the enterprise into a joint stock company in which the state retains a controlling share to enable it to continue applying the state policy with respect to the enterprise. If state property is transferred to the nongovernmental sector, ownership should be distributed over the broadest segment of the citizenry. This will incentivize the public's custodianship of public enterprises in which they have an ownership stake. The shareholding citizens will desire to maintain rather than lose such enterprises and to keep them beyond the control of politicians who would view such companies as spoils to be divvied up.

Privatization, which entails the transfer of ownership of public utilities to joint stock companies, is economically feasible and implementable on condition the state retains the authority to make economic decisions regarding the utility. There is no harm in the nongovernmental sector sharing ownership with the government and being responsible for operating the concerned utility.

Chapter 12

PUBLIC FINANCE REFORM

This road map addresses finance by emphasizing the need to provide incentives to the private sector to bear the burden of financing, modernizing, and developing public facilities. Private enterprise is the main engine of the national economy. It is the last resort for economic and social development and has a clear interest in such development. There is thus a need to address the objective reasons for the deepening mistrust between the political leadership and the business world.

The debate over public finance problems has become a political duel among parties who are mainly interested in exchanging accusations without referring to the root of the issue. They avoid treating the root causes and repercussions of such problems, as if addressing them was taboo. We do not claim to fully understand the complexities of public finance management, which is handled by multiple entities and is thus characterized by overlapping responsibilities, multiple outlooks, and conflicting policies and interests in the absence of a clear, binding governance strategy for our currently fragmented government.

In light of the above, we will briefly discuss a few topics to highlight the urgency of establishing a national strategy for reforming and managing public finance. Our aim here is to avoid the perils of continuing the current policy of overexpansion and risk-taking, which has bankrupted the government and depleted its resources. We will discuss the public debt scourge, tax reform, general budgeting methodology, and monetary policy.

The Public Debt Scourge

According to estimates of the International Monetary Fund, as of the end of 2014, the public debt reached a record high of $67.43 billion or 135 percent of GDP ($50 billion). However, this figure includes only treasury bonds and lines of credit issued by financial institutions. It does not include many other obligations owed by the state or state employee pension provisions, the net total of which is currently $20 billion.

The public debt has crossed the red line. It continues to grow amid the current economic slump; threatening Lebanon's paralyzed government with bankruptcy. Debt servicing, which totaled $4,380 million or 9 percent of GDP in 2014, imposes an unprecedented, unacceptable burden, particularly as interest rates on foreign currencies now hover around 1 percent, occasionally falling into negative territory.

Consecutive governments—perhaps lacking any alternative— have continued to borrow from the domestic banking sector at very high interest rates that reflect high credit risks. Lebanese banks, including the Central Bank of Lebanon, now hold 90 percent of Lebanese treasury securities, creating interdependence between the large banks and the government's financial position. The banks are totally dependent on the government's financial position. They cannot stop subscribing to treasury securities to extinguish or restructure outstanding debts. The annual average value of treasury security maturities during the next three years will exceed $15 billion, and the only recourse open to the state for dealing with this issue is to extinguish one debt with another, which will inevitably bankrupt the entire banking sector.

Faced with these imminent dangers, we cannot continue to view the public debt scourge as a necessary evil or incurable disease with which we must coexist until it kills us. To escape the deep hole we are in, we cannot simply wait for a miracle or persevere in the belief that restructuring or rescheduling the debt will solve the problem.

We cannot deal with the public debt scourge without addressing the root of the problem. Fleeing forward without a fundamental review of economic and financial policies and efforts to reduce interest owed on the debt would be futile.

It would also be futile to continue managing the public debt ad lib and without a strategy to reassure creditors regarding the credit risks of treasury securities. This cannot be achieved through the current policy unless we establish a separate public debt management fund, which would boost creditors' confidence in fiscal policy governance and existing guarantees of debt repayment.

Following are several ideas, though we do not claim to have an overarching view of the solutions needed:

- establishment of a separate public debt guarantee fund to be managed by a body comprising representatives of the Ministry of Finance, the Central Bank, Union of Banks, and others; and
- the financing of this fund with exceptional revenues and in-kind assets, including:
    - public assets that are neglected, usurped, or abandoned—such as maritime and riverine properties—and railways, roads, and passages that are no longer in service;
    - foreign aid from donor countries and Arab countries;
    - proceeds from the privatization of public utilities;
    - surplus generated by development activity;

- government savings in foreign exchange; and
- exceptional revenues from oil and gas, in case available, from the sovereign wealth fund.

Tax Reform

The imposition of taxes and fees is not intended solely to secure revenues for financing public expenditure. It is also intended to achieve the social objective of redistributing GDP more equitably, and the economic objective of developing economic activities and improving sectors and services that offer the highest social return.

In Lebanon, indirect taxes, which are imposed indiscriminately on all tax brackets, comprise the lion's share of tax revenues. Direct taxes, which are used to achieve fair, equitable distribution for the most disadvantaged groups, account for less than 20 percent of tax revenues. Consequently, the tax system is largely dysfunctional. The confessional system, which is culpable of the economic recession and faltering production, is notably responsible for the low percentage of direct tax collection.

Other reasons for low collection rates include:

- mistrust between taxpayers and the administration in general, which compels the overwhelming majority of taxpayers to doctor their books and conceal the financial position of their companies or businesses;
- unclear or sometimes contradictory tax laws and regulations, which cripple the initiative of tax officials seeking to be fair to taxpayers, particularly regulations pertaining to revenues from activities conducted outside Lebanon;
- taxpayers' shaky loyalty to the state. This is due to the substandard rating given by taxpayers to government performance and the paucity of benefits provided

by the state in exchange for the taxes and fees paid by taxpayers; and

- the tax comptroller lacking the authority to be fair to taxpayers. As a result, transparent taxpayers are punished, and taxpayers who are proficient at concealing or camouflaging their positions are rewarded.

The concentrated, earnest efforts made to institute tax reform and train staff assigned to administer the reform process, have not come to full fruition. The eagerly awaited political leadership will need to give top priority to tax reform, because it is the cornerstone for reforming public finance and establishing social justice.

General Budgeting Methodology

The methodology for general budgeting poses a problem that cannot be solved by the corrupt confessional system. The confessionalists view the budget as an official ledger for the distribution of shares as agreed among the confessional powers based on the balance of power, the relative size of the confessional groups, and popular lobbying in most cases.

In essence, the general budget is meant to set spending priorities based on the financial, economic, and social objectives expressed in the governance policy, which is binding on all parties. The budget becomes meaningless if it is not comprehensive, purposeful, and truthful in monitoring revenue and expenditure flows and covering the capital and operating expenditures of all public institutions.

The improvement of the framework and methodology for preparing general budgets, which are supposed to implement the economic vision of the government, must be a priority of the leadership that will be entrusted with the responsibility of ensuring economic development. We are accustomed to disregarding the drafting and passage of annual budgets; we are also used to the abdication of responsibility for controlling and ensuring the transparency of expenditures and monitoring the disbursement of public funds, all of which impedes the activity of the already hamstrung supervisory agencies.

Monetary Policy

Successive governments have adopted the policy of pegging the Lebanese pound to the US dollar regardless of economic conditions, GDP, competitiveness, cost of living, and the interest rate on the debt. However, it is not helpful at this time to question the soundness of this decision, which cannot be abandoned until the Lebanese economy is given a chance to recover.

The Lebanese economy has been dollarized. It is no longer possible, at least for the time being, to abandon dollarization without risk. The Central Bank is unable to play any effective role regarding the monetary situation. It cannot control interest rates on deposits and loans in dollars. Its role during the past fifteen years has been reduced to pegging the Lebanese pound to the US dollar at a huge cost to the national economy. It must be acknowledged that restoring the Central Bank's role, as defined by the law, particularly regarding monetary policy governance, must be put off until further notice.

A Final Word

The road map has heretofore not dealt with a number of issues and questions of public concern, particularly the following:

• Oil and Gas

We currently lack sufficient data to include hydrocarbon resources in the development plan. Lebanon's social and economic development resurgence may not need oil and gas if the country has wise leadership that can realize the potential of the country's unique riches, which are more important and better than oil and gas. In any case, if we cannot change the status quo, we will have no opportunity to exploit our hydrocarbon resources for the benefit of the economy and people, even if these resources could be extracted.

• The Problem of Displaced Syrians

Our economic reading of the situation does not address the displacement of Syrians to Lebanon. This displacement must be temporary. Lebanon cannot resettle any new refugees within its already crowded territory. The government which we hope will be established must act to prevent these displaced persons from receiving permanent asylum, regardless of the humanitarian or moral justifications. We cannot accept the settlement of additional displaced persons in Lebanon, lest we endanger Lebanon's survival.

Part III

FOR THE SAKE
OF LEBANON AS
A COUNTRY FOR
CULTURE AND LIBERTY

Introduction

L ebanon's raison d'etre is first and foremost to be a land of culture and liberty. Our small patch of land has long been a place where diverse cultures and civilizations have coexisted in a crucible of cross-pollination.

Culture and liberty must be the essence of any plan to reinvigorate the Lebanese nation. If not for its culture, Lebanon would not have found its prominent place in the world's consciousness. If not for the belief of Lebanese in their freedom and values, Lebanon would not have become a land of civilizations, and its mountains would not have been settled. These statements are not hyperbole and are in no way diminished by our current accelerating decline.

Culture is the noblest human pursuit. It embodies the legacy of civilizational evolution and refinement spanning multiple generations. It confers the characteristics of both creator and conqueror on the cultured person as he or she wages his or her legendary struggle for self-awareness and the realization of his or her humanity in the face of fear of the unknown.

Culture allows people to formulate essential, complex responses in their search for the meaning of their existence and in their efforts to be free of the constraints of time and place to exercise unencumbered freedom. Culture is humankind's best attempt at making sense of the biological, social, spiritual, and physical forces that shape our destinies.

If culture is the measure of civilization and progress, it is also a testament to the cultured person when he or she harnesses his or her will, thinking, and dreams to achieve human aspirations instead of exploiting the baser instincts of people to serve the usurpers of human dreams. When cultured intellectuals abdicate their responsibilities, rationality retreats and illusions take control, diverting society toward superstitious thinking, religious bigotry, and fanaticism; furthermore, society abandons the basic values of freedom, equality, human dignity, solidarity, and acceptance of others as brothers and sisters regardless of being different—a notion that had been entrenched by civilization throughout the ages.

Chapter 13

A UNIQUE CULTURAL HERITAGE

L ebanon did not evolve from a single culture, ethnicity, or language. In fact, it occupies a small corner of the Arab Mashreq with its vast deserts, where areas were once Assyrian, Babylonian, Persian, Egyptian, or Aramaic speaking. It is bordered by the sea of storms and pearls, the dwelling of Greco-Roman gods. Here, the Byzantine civilization, torn between Greece and Rome, still echoes, as do the tales of Cadmus, who offered the alphabet and abstraction as gifts to Europe, together with its own name, when he sailed there looking for his sister the Phoenician princess, the daughter of King Agenor, who had been kidnapped by Zeus to the west overseas.

Lebanon is a melting pot of human waves arriving from the sea and the desert. It may aptly be described as a unique spiritual and cultural crucible where East has met West since ancient times. Throughout history Lebanon has been a pathway, not so much for conquering armies as for human beings. Its coast served as a thoroughfare in the ancient world. There, and in its mountains, which were impervious to conquerors, the various spiritual and linguistic currents that have shaped human civilization interacted.

Returning to Lebanon's raison d'etre, we note that from its very inception, Lebanon—which was first settled by Phoenician sailors, who spread a culture of peace, knowledge, trade, art, taste, and aesthetics—has been more of a cultural crucible than a political or economic arena. Lebanon's very essence lies in the blending and interaction of its accumulated spiritual, linguistic, and intellectual layers, which have always been and will remain a cultural laboratory.

Lying astride the Mediterranean Sea and the desert, Lebanon evolved into a safe haven and oasis of freedom for religious and ethnic minorities. The interaction between these culturally, linguistically, and religiously diverse groups was not spontaneous. Rather, it was a conscious act on the part of the groups and individuals who fled from oases, coasts, and river banks elsewhere in the region to take refuge in Lebanon's mountains stronghold. They accepted a difficult subsistence existence as the price for freedom and human dignity. This geographically small area was thus transformed into a spiritual space whose dimensions went well beyond its geographical confines. Lebanon also became a meeting place for Christianity and Islam, the two main tributaries of Arab civilization. It evolved into a laboratory of unfettered coexistence, giving rise to a legacy that draws from multiple sources of inspiration, unencumbered and undistorted.

Some outcomes of this process are a unique heritage, peerless eloquence, a mélange of authenticity with modernity, and innovation of a special style in Arabic and other languages. This resulted in new linguistic, cultural, and civilizational dualities. Thus Lebanon found its own identity in a culture free of constraints; it drew upon the interaction and cross-pollination of the currents in making up its distinctive personality, and upon the harmonious existence of Islam and Christianity on its land in drawing up its message and role.

Chapter 14

A UNIQUE BLENDING OF MODERNITY WITH THOUGHT AND LITERATURE

It would be unusual for any scholar not to acknowledge the uniqueness of Lebanese culture, not only in the Arab world but throughout the world. No country subjected to so many events and changes has been able to survive as a bridge between disparate time periods for the conveyance of the legacy of human cultures.

Lebanon's cultural uniqueness emanates from its distinctive geographic, human, and historical characteristics. Inspired by the values of freedom, Lebanon's early diverse groups integrated, harmonized, and cross-pollinated with each other, exploring and mutually influencing each other. This process transcended the borders of the region and contributed to human culture in general. That would not have been possible without the Lebanese determination to reformulate their thought and expression and transcend the constraints of taboos to keep pace with modernity.

The Lebanese elites enthusiastically and prodigiously interacted with the revolutionary change in Western thought.

The popular revolts in Lebanon during the nineteenth century reflected that interaction, when early on they advocated for a republic and the separation of religion and state. We find what could be considered the basis of modern critical thought in the region in the writings of Farah Antoun and other nineteenth-century pioneers and later in the writings of Khalil Gibran, Ameen Rihani, Maroun Abboud, Constantine Zureiq, and many others. Lebanon, despite being a small country, distinguished itself throughout the Arab world as a leader in critical revivalist thought, and an advocate of liberation from the hegemony of religion and the religious establishment in the public domain. From Lebanon, the call for a tolerant Arabism free of sectarian affiliations was launched. Therein, contemporary thought in the Arab world took off together with the advocacy for democratic standards and a modern, secular, civil state free of outdated social traditions and constraints and committed to the values of freedom, justice, equality and solidarity.

The ambitions of the Lebanese elites transcended their small country. They traveled the globe, from Egypt to Europe, then to the Americas and all parts of the world. Everywhere, they sowed modern thought and Arab diaspora literature and poetry, which had a universal orientation. Through their efforts, Lebanon became much more than a corridor, bridge, or meeting forum. It became too prominent to be monopolized by a single religious community, religion, or ethnic group. These elites sought a shortcut to modernity and the entrenchment of democracy, justice, and freedom to avoid the costs and hardships of the slow, tortuous transformation that the West had experienced.

Chapter 15

THE LEBANESE INFLUENCE ON THE ARABIC LANGUAGE

The Lebanese elites played a vanguard role in the intellectual, literary, and artistic revolution that was launched in Beirut in the 1930s. This revolution took shape through insightful, purposeful initiatives to renew and modernize the Arabic language and Arabic literature in form and content. It was the culmination of the efforts of the founders of the renaissance to return the Arabs to their language and to revitalize knowledge of Arabic grammar and philology after a period of obscurantist Turkification.

In the early twentieth century, safe means of travel permitted the Lebanese cultural elites to become familiar with the Arabian deserts and to develop a sense of their special features. This enabled them to approach the corresponding diverse contents of thought, language, and the unending landscape, both real and imagined. Exposure to the geographical expanse of the Arab world gave these elites access to the Arab spirit and an understanding of the essence of its substance. It enabled them to skillfully liberate the Arabic language from the ruggedness of life in the desert without compromising its unique features and purity. They were thus able to enrich the Arabic language, make it more accessible, promote its broader usage and endow it with the global dimension it deserves.

Just as the Lebanese cultural elites have had a role in shaping the Arabic language, they also had a role in exposing the Arabic language to the languages of the world, especially French. This unique interaction among languages was never a goal in itself, but rather a vital link in the success of the Arab cultural renaissance, as it conferred a global character on that renaissance. Beirut, during the ten years preceding the civil war, was a unique international laboratory for the cross-pollination and harmonization of the Arabic language and culture with the values of freedom and modernity in global thought. It was also an international workshop for the translation and dissemination of universal thought and culture in the region.

Chapter 16

LEBANESE UNIQUENESS IN THE CULTURE OF LIVING TOGETHER

Lebanese society is a blend of peoples, ethnicities, cultures, and beliefs. In coming together they have been able, despite the independence and uniqueness of each one, to develop very distinctive features, and each group continues to be imbued with these features. This fusion has endowed each with a certain margin of the ability to transform and change. They are no longer insular. Their horizons are limitless. They have become able to coalesce around a cultural, intellectual enterprise that constitutes the unifying nerve of citizens, an enterprise whose goals transcend the borders of the small nation.

Humankind, now more than ever, needs a model culture of living together. The choice of the Lebanese founders for this model is not any more a purely Lebanese matter. Such a culture has become an existential need for the future of civilization and global stability, as highlighted by the demographic shifts entailed by the spread of religious, cultural, and ethnic diversity in most countries of the world as a result of the flow of immigrants from the poor southern countries into the rich West.

The cultural, humanitarian enterprise for which the Lebanese struggled in the last century sought to bring together the cultures of the East and West to interact, to familiarize different religions with each other, and promote dialogue. Their goal was to avoid descending again into the conflicts and wars that swept the old world, where, if one group sought to deny a neighboring group's right to be different, it would inevitably seek to forcefully eliminate or exclude that group or treat it as a subordinate minority.

Talk of Lebanon as an ideal laboratory for living together did not arise in a vacuum. Historically, none of the religious communities has ever oppressed any other religious community. Lebanon has been a shared haven for the groups that have settled in it during various historical periods in search of freedom, dignity, tolerance, and compassion. None of these groups wished to live in isolated ghettos. Once in Lebanon, they never were pervaded by any sense of being a subordinate minority or of having had their rights violated.

At least in its cultural dimension, Lebanon was the first to join the ideological trends that spread in the modern world. It was the first to turn against the past and its legacy after having absorbed and wedded the old with the new. Lebanon was the first to introduce and promote critical thought. It was the first to promote awareness of the need for modernization, change, and equality and freedom as fundamental necessities for living together and to protect against monopolistic and domineering tendencies.

Lebanon's founders believed the Lebanese nation to be greater than its geographic area or some collection of interests and quotas. They believed that this small entity would have no legitimacy unless it became a cultural and spiritual space and a safe haven for minorities fleeing from injustice and oppression. They believed that living together could not be sustained unless it was based on complete equality. They also believed that freedom would be incomplete unless each group refrained from trying to dominate other groups, and that the Lebanese nation would have no legitimacy or any role for its people unless it was transformed into a global laboratory for cultural dialogue and a place of freedom and modernity.

The Lebanese elites persisted in every stage of their struggle in calling for a secular civil state and a democratic republic free of factional oppression. They called for the separation of religion and state and the enactment of the controls to preclude a dictatorship of the majority. They called for a nation based on pluralism and on acceptance of the difference as an essential precept of the notion legitimacy.

Chapter 17

THE SHAKY GAMBLE

The leaders of the Renaissance bet on Lebanon as a cultural project that would extend to the entire region. Achieving this goal required establishing a state with the courage to acknowledge its modern identity and the obligations dictated by this identity, including a commitment to democratic values, valid representation, equality, alternation in exercising political power, preservation of individual freedom, human dignity, and the pursuit of social justice and economic development.

The cultural elites were not unaware that politics was key to the success and radiance of the cultural enterprise. A number of opinion makers in the nascent Arab states thus felt compelled to make serious forays into political activity. These attempts failed because they were at odds with the social legacy that the Ottoman sultanate left behind.

It was not impossible for the Lebanese state or neighboring states, after liberation from foreign occupation, to display a liberal, democratic, modern identity that did not contradict existing identities, which were either imagined or based on multiple inspirations. The political elites should have extracted what was shared and universal in these identities and employed that commonality to promote the embrace of unity amid diversity. But what happened was the complete opposite. The ruling families and their wobbly leaders sought to deepen the divisions and contradictions among identities to divide and control them in one way or another.

The Lebanese elites, despite suffering setbacks, were able to play a pioneering role. From the beginning of the nineteenth century, before states were formed, they were the most prominent advocates of democracy and republicanism in the Middle East. They witnessed the humble democratic experiences in the nascent entities that failed to develop or stabilize.

Clearly, these elites would not realize their ambitions unless their emerging states, whether Lebanon or the neighboring states, made some progress toward modernity. They expect these emerging states to be based on the nucleus of civil society with a degree of cohesion and loyalty to universal civilizational values, and moreover to aspire to build a national economy able to provide a measure of social protection for the neediest classes. The founders believed that the emerging Lebanese state's efforts to supply these three components augured well for a bright future. However, this promise was not to be realized, as the target ambitions were beyond the capacity of the political class who took power. This was true for a myriad of reasons, including the sectarian system, and the repercussions of regional developments, particularly the setback caused by the aggressive, racist Zionist enterprise.

The cultural elites in Lebanon and neighboring nascent Arab states were able to gain the admiration of the Lebanese and Arab bourgeoisie and the masses. But they could not at any time break into the political establishment that was holding the reins of power. That was similar to the case of military institutions and the tribal or family alliances, which were wary of direct conflict, and did not hesitate to stir up fears and passions to outflank any popular support for social progress and modernization ideas propagated by cultural elites. In that way, it distracted society, halting its movement toward progress and development.

After the radiant start of the spread of the call for republicanism and democracy, the cultural elites sought to take advantage of the experiences and achievements of Western societies in order to leapfrog ahead and come abreast of those societies. However, this effort failed despite its noble, earnest goals. Since the mid-nineteenth century, the feudalist powers had resisted the domestic popular movement led by Tanios Chahine calling for the establishment of a republic in Mount Lebanon. The feudalists' only means of countering the popular uprising was to exploit the fears and divisions that accompanied Ibrahim Pasha's campaign against Lebanon. Mount Lebanon was inundated with sectarian discord, contrary to its traditions. The discord was in part engineered by a coalition of forces with contradictory goals and motives, including the Ottoman sultanate, greedy European states eager to succeed the sultanate, local feudal lords, and aspirants to power.

Based on the pattern that led to the peasants' uprising led by Tanios Chahine, the fragmentation persisted. The political powers identified with the alleged interests of the religious communities, which usually led to the achievement of the objectives of the communities' leaders at the expense of their members. The country was thrown into internal divisions, which thwarted social cohesion, fragmented democratic thought, and precluded the emergence of a politically and morally fit political authority to extricate the country from its crises.

In 1958 tensions abroad led to a domestic crisis in Lebanon, which quickly morphed into sectarian disputes that lasted until direct international intervention created the conditions for the selection of Fouad Chehab as president. He was a wise, impartial, and patriotic leader. His government focused on establishing a stable state with modern institutions free of sectarian divisions, and qualified to handle legitimate social demands and provide the necessary platform for economic and social development. However, this experiment met with violent resistance on the part of the traditional family and tribal forces and the chaotic leaderships that were rising in the crisis-ridden Arab world. These factors combined to thwart President Chehab's experiment.

This setback undermined the institutions of the nascent state, which were usurped and transferred to religious communities and mafias allied with the sectarian leaders. Although this experiment was thwarted, it must be acknowledged that it was a serious, promising effort to rescue the state, and that could be tried again.

It may seem unrealistic to now talk of reviving a republic free of sectarian rending or to talk of reviving the Lebanese cultural enterprise after all the troubles and discord we have suffered. Attempts to establish such a republic and cultural enterprise have indeed faltered, but they still have a place in the hearts of Lebanese, and their structures remain intact. It must be remembered that the Lebanese cultural enterprise has proven its ability to resist attempts to fragment the country and divide it among the warring groups.

Despite attempts by foreign regimes and powers to mobilize and attract combatants to the civil war to tear apart the outwardly battered Lebanese entity, Lebanon has proven that it is more resistant to fragmentation and division than any other entity in the region. The Lebanese groups have never at any moment expressed, openly at least, a desire to abandon the democratic, republican system. All Lebanese continue to regard this system as the nurturer of their freedom and regulator of their covenants and precepts. We can claim that this system, though poorly implemented, is one of the few governing systems in our region that possess legitimacy.

The cultural arena is suffering from the immigration or resignation of a large segment of its vital actors. However, it still fosters a concentrated intense presence of cultural elites. This presence may be idle or marginalized, but that state of affairs cannot continue forever, and there has to be a state that believes that it derives its legitimacy from its culture.

Lebanon has been a cultural arena since antiquity. The cultural elites have constituted the cornerstone of the nation. They remain ready to participate in any serious attempt to revitalize, illuminate, and promote the national cultural project to achieve our people's ambitions. They share competence, experience, and a desire to meet and connect with each other. They are the ones able to use a common language to approach problems and disputes with reason, under the leadership of civil society that is capable of awakening our fragmented people, thus creating historical solutions for the crises brought about by our sectarian system, and formulating a modern secular republic to replace the sectarian system, which has proven resistant to reform.

Chapter 18

WHAT HAS HAPPENED, AND WHAT WILL HAPPEN?

The dramatic developments that have swept the Arab world and the accompanying brutal conflicts—which have been unparalleled in their intensity, futility, and contagiousness—are shedding light on the crisis in Arab societies, which are suffering from collective madness, thus making it possible to explain the causes of this unprecedented violence and to anticipate the future.

It was natural that culture would take center stage in Arab Spring events. Culture is commonly defined as "what is left over when everything is forgotten." This definition no longer suffices. In these times, which are teeming with complicated questions, culture has become the surest means of diagnosing the causes of our floundering, confused existence. The role of intellectuals, and the question of whether they are absent or detached, is no longer an incidental or private topic.

It is recognized philosophically that the universe becomes more complicated as it evolves and develops, that civilization becomes more open-minded, harmonious, and absorptive as it spreads and takes on additional accretions, and that humans move toward self-fulfillment. However, in our environment, at least outwardly, these trends are moving in the opposite direction. Many believe the Arab Spring stems from a conspiracy hatched by hostile parties to harm the Arab Spring countries. Only rarely does one encounter a treatment of the real reasons for the popular uprisings and their violent turn, namely the acute imbalances in our brittle social structures and the unprecedented existential repercussions of a historically unprecedented scientific revolution that is affecting peoples laboring under imposed backwardness, ideological terrorism, and isolationism.

There exists a sharp disparity in development patterns within the Arab Spring countries. On the one hand, material life is changing rapidly due to the information technology revolution; on the other hand, intellectual stagnation, which has ideological and cultural dimensions, has prevailed in the Arab Spring countries due to certain sociological and political characteristics which they all share. The resulting structural imbalance has engendered greater fears among marginalized individuals over the emerging vacuum. This vacuum cannot be addressed purposefully in societies that have been emptied of their cultural and existential defenses by destructive forces. Such forces use agencies of crude oppression to transform citizens into puppets controlled by an extremist chauvinist rhetoric or austere demagoguery. The robbing of citizens of their dignity, freedom, and minds has left them easily exposed to indoctrination by Salafist groups and spontaneous subscription to fundamentalist ideology as a means of addressing their fears and channeling their resentment.

The acute social differences among citizens within a single country—which stem from corrupt, failed economic policies—have led to huge income and wealth distribution gaps, which have steadily widened the social gap between individuals, classes, regions, groups, and religious communities, and created a new social reality characterized by backwardness, oppression, and withdrawal.

This new, unjust social reality could not last forever. It could not withstand the bubbling resentment generated by deprivation and humiliation. It was liable to explode at the first opportunity available to citizens to impede or confront the machine that was brutally repressing them. Senegalese president and poet Léopold Senghor, contemporaneous with the rapid social transformations in the African continent and the accompanying structural disequilibria, referred to this dilemma in an interview with the French newspaper *Le Monde* in March 1982, wherein he points out that stability and sustainability are not possible in any new economic and social order that is not preceded by a new cultural order. This sequence did not play out in the countries that declared war on their intellectuals and made culture and thought cardinal taboos.

The military cliques that seized power in the Arab Spring countries hastened to wipe clean society's memory and uproot its cultural legacy. That legacy of accumulated wisdom and tolerance evolved through many centuries of experiences. It anchored a firm, cohesive system of social relations that survived even the darkest of times and managed to preserve unity, harmony, and the living together among the people. The cliques that usurped power had no social legacy on which to stand, nor were they far-sighted. They believed they could monopolize power forever. They systematically sought to exclude or eliminate the role of traditional social leaders or to even physically eliminate them. They sought the help of repressive apparatuses to achieve their goals under the cover of spurious slogans calling for modernization, renewal, and the combating of reactionism. But they did so only to exclude the national bourgeoisie, which threatened their shameless, savage rape of the land and of memory. The best weapon of these cliques was exploitation of the centrality of the Palestinian issue and the struggle with Zionism to justify calling for assimilating into an imagined inclusive homogeneous society, devoid of differences, paralyzed and helpless. This policy deprived Arab societies of their traditional, inherited sources of moral authority, which had preserved the pluralism and unity of society. As a result, Arab societies have been left prey to despair and emptiness.

The key challenge for Arab intellectuals was to have the desire and ability to demonstrate a distinctive Arab identity that is open to modernity and democracy instead of the regressive, fatalistic, exploitable identities that were harbored or imagined. The regimes that seized power, and the culture they sought to implant, resorted to obliterating people's identity and moral authority figures. They replaced them with the ruler's identity and the values represented through his followers within the government apparatuses, tribes, and the crowds of sycophants, beneficiaries, and corrupt careerists. Naturally, the emptying of society of its leaders and authority figures would lead to the rehabilitation of extremist, fanatical ideologies on whose behalf religion is made to bear false witness to justify deviance and greed for power. These ideologies have employed history as a reservoir of resentment by using simple people's grudges against their rulers.

Everything that has happened took place while intellect or intellectuals have had no role or presence. Our stricken societies have had no chance of reclaiming their memories and reconciling with their history. Meanwhile, what will happen and the manner in which it will take place, depends on the return of the Arab intellectuals from their withdrawal, and their regaining of their courage to criticize. This also depends on Lebanon's reclaim of its pivotal role in leading the march to reclaim thought and prepare for a new renaissance in a world that must choose between culture and decay.

Chapter 19

THE PROMISE THAT IS STILL A DREAM

On April 15, 1970, the Lebanese Council of Ministers headed by President Charles Helou decided to approve a UNESCO project to build an international human sciences center in the ancient city of Byblos. The council took note of an offer by Dr. Manuel Younes to donate the necessary land for the construction of the center.

Manuel Younes was a visionary professor of philosophy who had returned from abroad to achieve a dream that had preoccupied him from his early youth throughout his whole life. He found an ally and partner in Maurice Gemayel, who had the same vision and ambition. The two were able to convince UNESCO of the project's importance.

UNESCO justified its decision to undertake the project because of "Lebanon's distinct culture and location between Asia, Africa, and Europe, which has made it a meeting place for the civilizations of the West and the East. Moreover, the historical city of Byblos is a symbol as the birthplace of the alphabet and the city of the book. We appreciate the position of the Lebanese government, which has repeatedly expressed its commitment to preserving Lebanon's unique cultural heritage, distinctive features, and global cultural presence."

Manuel Younes and Maurice Gemayel were not alone in seeking to transform this unique and inspiring corner of Lebanon into an international cultural center and an academy for human sciences that reflects the human need to transcend ethnicity, religion, and culture. It was decided that the center would include a university specializing in the humanities. The university would be open to the world. It would promote cross-cultural dialogue and serve as a meeting place where cultures and civilizations could become familiar with each other, interact, cross-pollinate, and foster mutual inclusion. Additionally, there was to be a global interreligious forum to allow all religions to become familiar with each other, as well as a conference center offering a platform for Byblos's message to the three continents and the world as a whole.

The founders' dream turned into a broad cultural movement with the participation of many prominent thinkers at the time, including, from Lebanon, the philosopher René Habachi, Hassan Saab, Michel Asmar, Hassan Mucharrafieh, Salah Steitieh, Butrous Dib, Edmond Rizk, Karim Pakradouni, Therese Salameh Zaarour, and others. The project also had the support and enthusiasm of such figures as Pablo Neruda, Bruno Kreisky, and several leaders of international organizations. In 1973, National Education Minister Edmond Rizk and UNESCO director general René Maheu signed an agreement based on UNESCO resolution 453EX93, which assigned UNESCO to manage the center in cooperation with Lebanon.

However, the dream remained only a promise that was dashed by the sordid civil war—a war wherein people served as tools and fuel and in which our own land was transformed into a battlefield. The promise became a nightmare reminiscent of a ceremonial mass suicide. We ignored the promise of culture, the world's existential need for the culture of living together, and our mission to the region and the global village, which is still seeking its humanity. We struggled over identities that have yet to be reconciled with ourselves. We became divided over creeds. We distorted those creeds and imbued them with our own purposes, delusions, and fears. We fought over loyalties and affiliations, over war and peace, over capitalism and Marxism. We traded our thoughts for instincts. We plunged ourselves into the depths of emptiness and aversion. In the end, what happened is that the founders passed away one after the other. The determination of the frustrated intellectuals faded. Lebanon's status and cultural splendor retreated. UNESCO chose to step away from the global dimension of the project and classified it as a second-tier cultural project. It limited its role to moral oversight contrary to what had been previously decided. In 2013, the center's board appointed Dr. Adonis al Akra as director general. On May 1, 2013, he took up his duties in a modest building in Byblos's old city with extremely modest resources.

The European, African, Asian, and Arabic-speaking worlds need to revive this project and implement it as originally planned. This is possible if Lebanon has political and cultural leaders who have the desire and determination to restore the nation to its place at the forefront of the modernization, transformation, and democratization processes in the agonized Middle East, which is still waiting for distinguished leaders of a second renaissance and continues to dream of an international center for the humanities in Byblos that can illuminate a world searching for its lost self and for balance.

Chapter 20

THE RESTORATION OF LEBANON AS A CULTURAL HUB

Our remarks about culture are intended to emphasize its pivotal role in reclaiming the nation and reviving it politically, economically, and socially. The revival must be accompanied and regulated by a cultural renaissance. Culture provides society with the necessary inviolability and cohesion in facing the tensions and contradictions resulting from rapid developments and changes. This second renaissance will not occur unless scholars, philosophers, authors, poets, and artists mobilize all their energies to provide safe passage for the republic. The republic in turn will derive its legitimacy from its own modern values and from its embrace of society's legacy, heritage, and pluralistic, humanitarian, open-minded identity, which must be liberated from sectarian and religious fanaticism.

Culture echoes the pulse of life and human feelings and awareness of existence vis-à-vis nature, the Creator, and other humans. The cultural project to which we aspire transcends our fates and the geography of our nation. It cannot be limited to definitions or words. It is the future promise of the republic. It is contingent on the will and courage of Lebanon's intellectuals to achieve this promise and to restore our nation as a cultural hub.

It is also contingent on whether the state will decide to provide the basic factors of the renaissance, the most important of which are:

- Freedom: Culture at the bottom is absolute freedom. Culture cannot be limited in its ambit. It cannot exist without freedom. Freedom must be faultless and unfettered. It must extend to every individual's thought, beliefs, and position on society and life.

  Responsibility for defending freedom is shared by the state and the intellectuals themselves. The state must first believe in the values and notions of freedom, discharge its responsibilities, and exercise its right to use legitimate violence to enforce the law and deter those who would transgress against people's freedom, the natural world, and life. Intellectuals are the custodians of freedom, not only of their own freedom but also of the freedom of those who differ with them in their opinions, beliefs, and convictions. Intellectuals also promote the culture of responsible freedom, which seeks to avoid conflict with the rights of others or with the values of the republic.

- The cultural environment: In order to grow, blossom, and thrive, culture needs a nurturing environment, light, and air, like any living thing. The state must provide intellectuals with the necessary atmosphere and resources to launch Lebanon's cultural enterprise. The state's policy must incorporate an awareness of culture being at the forefront of foundational values. It must recognize that investment in culture in this age bears greater economic yield than any other investment, and that freeing intellectuals from need and time constraints, to permit them to fully unleash their creative energies, may offer a return that far exceeds that of investments in any other field.

The provision of a nurturing environment for culture is a paramount responsibility of the republic and the political elites. The implementation of a resplendent, sustainable cultural project is the responsibility of the intellectuals themselves. They must adhere to the requirements of integrity in practices entailed by their cultural pursuits. This in turn is reflected in their own self-respect and the respect of others. They must be keen on the integrity of their responsible, courageous, critical thought, which is the most accurate measure for evaluating the mission and sustainability of culture.

- The natural environment and landscape: The ongoing wars and semi-wars, which have deprived us of the past forty years, have inflicted irreparable damage on Lebanon's landscape, natural environment, and architectural and cultural heritage. This sinful destruction has not been limited to the physical environment; it has also extended to good taste, aesthetic sense, architecture, antiquities, and public utilities. It has contributed to frustration, marginalization, emigration, and the diminishment of the role of most intellectuals. It has also obliterated the cultural memory, transformed education into a commercial business, and debased the arts, reducing them to moneymaking ventures.

Some believe the disfigurement, destruction, and other outcomes, together with the accompanying exorbitant devastation and deliberate savagery toward the scenery could not have occurred spontaneously solely due to greed and the absence of intellectual and moral leadership. They believe that these acts were also reactions driven by the suppressed resentment among broad segments of the public toward the failed political power which across the board has in effect declared Lebanon's natural environment to be fair game for destruction and disfigurement. The political leadership for which Lebanon hopes must be aware of this catastrophe and its impact on the economy, society, and culture. It must take quick, decisive measures to stop the destruction and address the disfigurement, based on an ambitious public advisory plan prepared by Lebanese and international experts with demonstrable competence.

Repairing the damage of the assault on nature and public and private property requires massive investments, the most urgent of which could exceed five billion dollars. These investments are reasonable compared to the direct economic return that will redound to the benefit of various economic sectors and to Lebanon's moral standing and cultural enterprise.

The intellectuals for their part must be aware of their responsibilities in furthering the artistic, literary, and cultural renaissance. The renaissance will for the most part be judged by its ability to put back into circulation the aesthetic capital that has been accumulated by generations of Lebanese. It will also be judged by its ability to restore the enchanting landscape and regulate the general aesthetic view and ensuring good taste in architecture and urban development.

In order for Lebanon to be a strong beacon, there is no substitute for culture.

Lebanon was never greater or more brilliant than when it was home for Arab intellectuals, liberals, and opponents of ignorance and tyranny, when Beirut, with its universities and publishing houses, was the metropolis of the Arab world and a radiant hub of renaissance thought, literature, art, poetry, and song. It was never greater than when it addressed the Arabs in an eloquent Lebanese tongue, held dialogue with the West in its languages, and was conversant with its ideas and concerns.

The people of Lebanon were never greater than when they were pioneers of social advancement and knowledge for themselves and others and those who could affirm the values of modernity for their countries. They were at their peak when their elites were a guiding light for the formation and entrenchment of these values in daily life as a way to maintain human dignity, liberty, and the right to disagree or be different.

At this time of deep frustration, amid the dissolution brought on by the blind system of apportionment and sectarianism, our remarks here might seem strange or delusional were it not for the testimony of those who have steadfastly resisted the sectarian, tribal, and surveillance cliques. These cliques have assailed Lebanon with their fanaticism, pestilence, and deviance and schemed to transform it into a laboratory of death and despair in their vile aspiration to destroy the one and only democratic enterprise in the Arab world that is based on diversity and respect for pluralism. Had it not been for our culture, our crisis-ridden, desolate society could not have resisted the impious hatred, which it did with hope and pride despite the pain. Nor would it have maintained the promise enshrined in the following verses of *Cadmus* by the late poet Said Akl: "My country, the one that remained faithful albeit treated with ingratitude. Lebanon is a covenant. My country is not cedars, mountains, or water; my country is love—there is no room for hatred within love."

When speaking of the tragedy that overshadows us today, and of Said Akl's promise to Cadmus, the teacher of Greece of yore, which today is drowning in financial and subsistence crises and in the humdrum of life in its ancient cities dedicated to the spirits and the gods, it would be pleasant to return to the night of the ancient city of Thebes, which is haunted by the legends of Cadmus and Oedipus, and where the voice of Antigone still rings out: "'I was born to share love, not hate."

Antigone, immortalized by Sophocles twenty-five centuries ago, is still a major attraction at theaters around the world, remade by giants of modern drama such as Jean Cocteau, Jean Anouilh, Bertolt Brecht, and others. This young woman, the daughter of Oedipus and Jocasta, still arouses the passion of leading philosophers to explore the depths of humanity. The philosopher Hegel hallows Antigone as "the noblest of figures who ever appeared on earth," whereas Martin Heidegger drew on her personality in making his most important conclusions about human nature and its terrible deviations.

In the gifts that Greece gave to global culture we find the secret of the Greek people's pride amid their ordeal, and we find an explanation for the strength which has enabled the Greek government to resist the arrogant financial powers. It would be accurate to say that the writer Sophocles, who lived 2,500 years ago, has had a greater hand in Greece's steadfastness and strength than Prime Minister Tsipras. What is valid for Greece may also explain Lebanon's steadfastness during the storm.

Culture provides a unifying myth for societies that contend with ethnic, religious, or cultural diversity. For Lebanon, culture is the only way to reanimate its human laboratory, which is indispensable to the dissemination of a culture of living together among Muslims and Christians—who represent more than half of the world's population—both in the stricken Middle East and in our tottering world at large.

Gambling on reviving Lebanon's role in these stormy times and spreading a culture of familiarity and interaction between the Islamic and Christian civilizations has become an existential need for ensuring the stability of many countries and for confronting the destructive violence in the Middle East and the barbaric tendency toward negation and exclusion in other countries.

If culture is Lebanon's raison d'etre, it is only natural for cultural values to be paramount within the larger set of values of the future civil republic. A value system founded upon the nation's cultural heritage is the linchpin determining the success of the fateful gamble on Lebanon's role and in maintaining the continued sympathy and understanding that the small nation still enjoys. Culture and freedom justify Lebanon's existence.

Conclusion

WHITHER THE CIVIL MOVEMENT (AL-HIRAK AL-MADANI)?

We are anew at a historic moment and I was trying to lean on my intellect together with my experiences of a lifetime to come up with a road map for regaining the civil state that was ravished on the very day it was born. The French obstetrician had exchanged it with a semi-hybrid state whose genetic composition includes sectarian genes that impair its functioning and development.

In my book, *The Other Lebanon,* I mentioned that there is no way we can regain it unless we have the courage to free ourselves from the confinement of our confessions and obsessions and unless we decide to live together equitably and in harmony, without giving up on our precepts, conventions, and covenants. In that book I also made clear that the easiest and most secure way to reach this goal is through completing the implementation of the provisions of the Taif Agreement, which had put an end to the vile war. This agreement has decreed relinquishing the sectarian formula of our political system; meanwhile, charging the Lebanese themselves, with no need for any protection or mandate, with the responsibility of looking for an alternative formula that suits them. This alternative formula has to be suited for rescuing their country from backwardness and obstruction, safeguarding it, and reinforcing its role as a human laboratory and meeting space for cultures and religions wherein they can get to know each other and live together.

In this book I have expressed a point of view, namely that the failure and humiliation that we suffer from in our national life is nothing but the inevitable outcome of a political system which is corrupt by nature.I have expressed the ability of our people to achieve the economic and cultural miracle that we have wasted. This miracle still has a chance for resurgence provided that this fettered republic could free itself from a system inherently bound to conflict among its constituencies, and within each of them. This inevitability of conflict is not due to lack of competence of the political establishment, but due to the fact that the survival of the regime requires a continuous conflict among these constituencies.

I have emphasized the indispensable role of the president, a role entrusted to him by Article 95 of the Constitution to head the National Dialogue Committee, which is counted upon to come up with a nonsectarian formula to replace the actually condemnable sectarian system. Therein I expressed despondence, given the fact that all those who assumed responsibility as presidents shirked the constitutional provisions they took an oath to abide by. I clarified the reasons that pushed me to believe that there is no way out of this void unless the presidency regains its role and duties, and civil society regains its vigor. Civil society has to mobilize toward pressuring for the formation of a national dialogue committee. The committee needs to comprise of select and reliable intellectuals, profoundly cultured and scientific-minded, thus well suited for drafting a clear, honest, and purposeful social covenant for living together. This contract is expected to replace the ailing confessional quota system of which we are witnessing the final stage in its struggle to survive.

The civil society movement or the popular uprising, witnessed lately in the streets of the capital city, Beirut, is not a transient event, or some case of protest against corruption or any of its many issues. Given its radicality, wide dispersion, and momentum, it seems to reflect a growing consciousness within the youth milieu—in universities and among social and cultural elites that are afflicted by the confessional quota system. I admit that this event or movement has not surprised me much. For a long time, I have expected certain developments that may facilitate breaking through the comprehensive void which had been brought about by the quota system in its latest version named as consensual democracy. This fad theoretically entails an inconceivable agreement on the apportionment of extensive fiefdoms among parties with a dubious nature and conflicting interests. This apportionment is based on ambiguous criteria posed by forces with a shifting balance of power. Practically this transforms the public sphere into estates contested by different powers representing the religious communities. These powers may as well take hold of these estates forcibly through an apportionment of spoils; or they may abuse them as if they are entitled here to the rights of an owner vis-à-vis his or her own property.

I have been certain that the system crisis is no more manageable, and that eventually it will lead into its disintegration. Recently, I became convinced that one or several parties in the ruling sectarian establishment, itself, behave as if driven by a conscious plan that they have concocted to bring about a total deactivation of the confessional quota system. This implies toppling the state and going back to civil wars, unless, as the Taif Agreement stipulated, a formula for an alternative system is effected; a system which allows for a peaceful democratic evolution of our political institutions.

Prior to 1975, civil society had a considerable effect on public life. To a good extent it used to play the role of a countervailing power which kept an eye on the ruling establishment, thereby setting right its deviations as much as possible. It used to lean on a system of human values emanating from the deeply entrenched rural highland cultural heritage, and from the modern values of urban bourgeoisie with a touch of idealist leftist ideology. This civil society used to weigh the political establishment according to the generally accepted moral values. It used to despise brokers and those who get rich through deals; and reject the corrupt and those who take bribes. Meanwhile, politicians used to have limited riches, and their transgressions used to take place secretly and timidly out of fear of public opinion, mobilizing the people, and the judiciary. Though the management of public affairs was not sound or ideal, it used to abide by the dictum "if you were inflicted by sins, then try to be discreet."

During the period of Syrian tutelage in Lebanon, in the wake of the Lebanese Civil War, the role of civil society was totally excluded and weakened. The idealist value system that existed in the milieu of the youth has been terribly distorted. Religious communities have relentlessly subdivided the youth, humiliated them, and impelled them to immigrate. They pushed them into conformity with the opportunistic and nihilist patterns of behavior of the contingent tutelage society. Corruption became a form of cleverness, whereas violating and usurping the public sector became shrewdness. Meanwhile, bribery turned into a legitimate sectarian revenue. The supervisory and cross-questioning role of civil society was damaged, and the possibility of a public protest was defused; it was rendered sectarian and subordinate. This allowed the apportionment system to unmask its hideous face.

It had been obvious that the weak authority, which ruled after the retreat of the tutelage era, was unable to satisfy the most basic needs of young generations in universities and marginalized masses. They were brought down by the apportionment system, which is subordinate to clientelism, henchmen, and faithful supporters. It was only natural for these forces, which suffered exclusion for a long time, to mobilize thus facing the institution that was responsible for their exclusion. However, the outcome of the uprisings in Lebanon's neighboring countries was not encouraging for demanding an overthrow of the confessional quota system; it was feared that this may topple the state and undermine the little left of its symbolic existence. What did not seem obvious here was the extent to which civil society complied with the position of some in that movement who called for overthrowing the system. Also, it was not clear the readiness or tendency of the civil society to sympathize with the system and protect it despite the tragedies and failures that the Arab uprisings have brought about.

In fact, the mismanagement of the solid waste problem, though it instigated the movement, alone it could not explain its breadth and intensity. The deals that this solid waste issue entails do not exceed $200 million per year. In addition, the scale of its underlying corruption seems minimal once compared with that related to other considerably large-scale issues of corruption such as the one related to electricity whereby mismanagement results in a budget deficit exceeding $4 billion yearly. Added to this debt, consumers incur direct expenses such as paying for complementary sources of electricity generation, and indirect expenses emanating from the stagnation in the national economy that results from the electricity problem. In fact, the problem of solid waste should not have been tough or thorny. During the early 1970s, through an initiative taken by Kamal Joumblat, Beirut municipality constructed in its solid waste dumpsite a factory for waste management (sorting, organic fermentation, and incineration of the refuse). This factory was the first of its kind in the Middle East, with the latest technology then; actually, it is still in existence and is fit for rehabilitation. Yet conflict of interest between powerful groups, similar to the case of other deals, has led to a chaotic management of the solid waste issue. Thus, after a prolonged tardiness in finding a solution to this waste issue, and at a point where it was no more possible to ignore addressing it, public opinion assumed that a deal and an apportionment has taken place regarding it between the parties of the sectarian establishment. Concomitantly, public opinion was aware that this same establishment is unable to find solutions for pivotal matters the struggle over which has led to disabling the state, thus making its institutions inoperative, damaging its security and economy, and mortgaging the future of its coming generations. It was the presumed agreement and apportionment among the parties of the confessional establishment in the matter of solid waste which provoked the enthusiasm of the youth. It led them to express their indignation at the confessional quota system which is responsible for their suffering. Hence, corruption in the case of solid waste management was not at the core of the movement.

Despite the diversified slogans of the groups in the movement, and regardless of the extent to which their lack of experience may limit their ability to determine or unify their goals, the central goal of the movement remains evident. This movement has clearly declared its hostility to the confessional quota system. It considers this system a tool used by powerful positions within religious sects in order to monopolize the public realm to their own advantage and that of their followers and proponents, and in order to marginalize the youth force and exclude it from the sphere of decision making. This has pushed the youth into the streets, thus expressing their anger at the system and contesting its rendering corruption an inevitable destiny due to its very structure, whereby sectarian apportionment persists.

For the first time in a long time, the street is no more a frontier for sectarian entities, a barricade or border, or a field for a show of force. The heart of Beirut is a square where people get together; a place consecrated to the future and not meant to uphold memories of the past with the contradictions of religious groups. Civil society, which was scattered and decimated in 1975, has come back to life and is announcing its refusal to be invested in conflicts of sectarian positions which compete over its own subsistence and dignity. Civil society also aims at maintaining that it still is capable of changing the rules of the game and bringing about a reshuffle, thereby moving from an instinctual sectarian allegiance to a nonsectarian one. This is the first time in Lebanese history that social grouping takes place according to this rule, through a spontaneous initiative. This initiative emanated from marginalized popular circles which had the courage to proclaim their intention to exercise their role as an effective and independent party or player—an independence from all other political formations, political parties, organizations, and groups which have lost their legitimacy whenever they were biased toward one of the sectarian groups.

The revival of civil society, which calls for the establishment of a modern state on the wreckage of the confessional quota system, has led those powers that profited from the apportionment of spoils to be wary of the civil society movement, as it represents popular legitimacy and moral inviolability. This pushed the political establishment to deal with it cautiously and equivocally in the hope of containing it or having some of its groups become followers to one of the groups or parties of this establishment. It also hoped to divert the movement from its main goals and distract it with side issues that do not touch upon the root of the problem, namely the confessional quota system itself. These powers that have a stake in this system benefited from the poor coordination and the aimless actions of certain factions of the movement, and from the attempts by certain political parties, obsolete organizations, and public figures to retrieve their illusions and dogmatic discourse. Yet most of the factions of the movement intended to bravely and candidly announce their independence from and hostility toward the confessional quota system, and called for its downfall. They expressed clearly their identity as an agglomeration of civil nonsectarian forces, opposed to sectarian thought that has monopolized the political space since the end of the tutelage era.

The uprising that has mainly crystallized in July 2015 may subside for some reason, but it will eventually return to the streets with more determination, better organization, and a greater ability to fight a decisive battle for peacefully overthrowing the confessional quota system. Triumph in such a pivotal confrontation may require increased awareness, planning, and perseverance. The movement needs to draw lessons from the current practices of the uprising, given its mistakes and setbacks. These lessons are important to consolidate its consciousness and facilitate defining its goals and designing its strategy for achieving them. The lessons should be based on experience derived from social facts, the most important of which is that the principle of nonsectarian grouping elicits an unexpected extensive public sympathy; for a better future, this situation needs to continue and become more entrenched and able to generate a social environment where it is fostered by the public.

However, there has to be no mix-up between overthrowing the sectarian system and overthrowing the state—also, no confusion of using the street as a space for expressing the national will for a peaceful change, with using it as a space for venting hatred and vandalizing public and private property. The youthful nature of the civil society movement has brought about mistakes or missteps associated with chaotic conduct of some irresponsible and immature elements, pointing accusatory fingers to directions unconnected to the goals of the uprising, and a weak strategy coupled with diverse propounded issues that almost eclipsed the main cause of the uprising—namely, overthrowing the confessional quota system.

In fact, the most serious danger that may jeopardize the future of the uprising and deny it popular embrace lies in distracting it with unsolvable futile side issues so as to thwart it, induce a clash with it, push it to vent its outrage in the streets, and overlook the main goal of the movement. Accordingly, what is the objective of demanding the resignation of a minister who seems to be too absent or that of a head of an organization who is present? What instrumentality should be employed for combating corruption when the political system is intrinsically corrupt? Is it appropriate to blame economic and social deterioration on the productive enterprising private sector so as to turn a blind eye to the flaccid corrupt state institutions and their guardians—bullies, middlemen, and profiteers?

What is the point of targeting the ruling political establishment and holding it accountable for corruption, dependency, and deterioration, if it were not to vindicate the apportionment system? What is the use of wasting time on an exaggerated or oversimplified discourse on this chaotic, fragmented, and collapsing institution, by considering it a closed organization with a class consciousness of its own? Perhaps this belief is true to a certain extent, taking into consideration the political class that ruled in the wake of independence. Yet the ruling class has changed drastically after the Lebanese Civil War started, where most of the power positions assumed earlier by certain families had moved to new leaderships that came into existence through war circumstances or through the will of the tutelage power. Actually, corruption has become more entrenched and apportionment more virulent; on the other hand, it has become rare to notice any of the representatives of the political establishment avoid criticizing the system, or refrain from announcing his complaint about its repercussions, or from convicting it and expressing the wish to abandon it. Claims of solidarity and coordination among the sectarian parties contradict reality. It goes without saying that the political class within the booby-trapped consensual democracy system is bound to be in conflict from within. This permanent and exhausting struggle encourages power positions within the sectarian establishment to give up the apportionment system once it finds in the alternative system a way out of the inescapable existential crisis.

Finally, I would like to address the young men and women of the civil society movement who represent the promise of a civil republic returning to the state, loaded with culture, freedom, and joy. I appeal to you for sharing my profound belief that the future of your country, and its unique humanistic role in the radiance of the culture of living together, depend on your courage, wisdom, and cleverness in promoting an atmosphere of a popular embracement of a complete implementation of the Taif Agreement. This will set the stage for the start out of the Lebanese laboratory wherein civilizations and cultures meet, get to know each other, and come to be on familiar terms.

I am glad to confirm to you my conviction that the current circumstances, both domestically and internationally, no matter how tangled and dismal they may seem, are more favorable than any time in the past to free ourselves from the confinement of our system and our religious communities. I believe that counting on success in the battle for a democratic peaceful change is a winning bet.

Counting on regaining the nation and the future of its generations depends on your ability to keep abreast with the process of change. This process is highly dependent upon the leadership, resolve, and vision of a president who has the potential to make history. Then it gets moving after the formation of the National Dialogue Committee with select reputable members. The process leads to victory together with your movement, which is geared toward founding a popular embracement for a thought free from intolerance, racism, or sectarianism.

I am delighted to count on your will, which yields change, with the mastermind that sets up an efficient path, and on the wisdom pronounced by poet Al-Mutanabbi, "The mind has priority over courage."

www.ingramcontent.com/pod-product-compliance
Lightning Source LLC
Chambersburg PA
CBHW030433290526
45786CB00001B/273